THE CHANNEL ISLANDS

BLACK'S
POPULAR
SERIES of
COLOUR
BOOKS

∇

VOLUMES IN THE SERIES

Other Volumes to follow

AGENTS

AMERICA . . . . . THE MACMILLAN COMPANY
64 & 66 FIFTH AVENUE, NEW YORK

AUSTRALASIA . . . OXFORD UNIVERSITY PRESS
205 FLINDERS LANE, MELBOURNE

CANADA . . . . . . THE MACMILLAN COMPANY OF CANADA, LTD.
ST. MARTIN'S HOUSE, 70 BOND STREET, TORONTO

INDIA . . . . MACMILLAN & COMPANY, LTD.
MACMILLAN BUILDING, BOMBAY
309 BOW BAZAAR STREET, CALCUTTA
INDIAN BANK BUILDINGS, MADRAS

ST. PETER-PORT, GUERNSEY, FROM THE POOL.

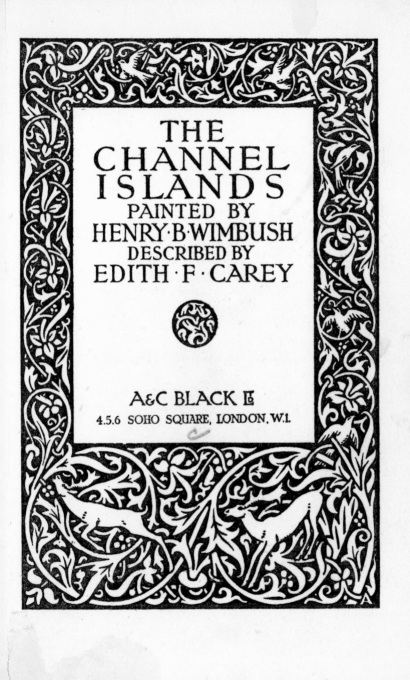

THE CHANNEL ISLANDS

PAINTED BY
HENRY·B·WIMBUSH
DESCRIBED BY
EDITH·F·CAREY

A&C BLACK LD
4.5.6 SOHO SQUARE, LONDON, W.1.

First Edition, with 76 illustrations, published in 1904

Second Edition, with 32 illustrations, published in 1924

Printed in Great Britain by
BILLING AND SONS, LTD., GUILDFORD AND ESHER

PREFACE

In this second edition of my book on the Channel Islands I have perforce had to cut down the original volume by about forty pages; this volume was written twenty years ago, and in twenty years many changes have happened in the Islands, and I also—I hope—have learned more about them. Therefore, many alterations and modifications have been made in the text, and whole chapters have been re-written, but the original scheme has been adhered to; namely, an attempt merely to sketch the history of Jersey, Guernsey, Alderney, and Sark, pointing out a few of the many legends and traditions associated with them, the storm and stress through which they have battled, some of the remnants of feudalism which they have managed to preserve, and certain conspicuous men and women who once lived in them. I trust, therefore, that nobody will open the book in the hope of obtaining from it any useful information with regard to the trade, the agriculture, the natural history, or the geological formation of the Channel Islands. Mr. Wimbush has painted them as they are—bathed in sunshine, radiant with flowers, busy and well-to-do in this pros-

Preface

perous if prosaic age. I have tried to recall "le souvenir des beaux jours envolés" of these "morceaux de France tombés à la mer et ramassés par l'Angleterre," as Victor Hugo calls them.

For my facts, so far as they are taken from printed books, I am indebted mainly to the following writers:—

DUPONT, *Histoire du Cotentin et de ses Iles* (Caen, 1870).

DE LA CROIX, *Jersey, ses Antiquités, ses Institutions, son Histoire* (Jersey, 1861).

   ,,   ,,   *La Ville de St. Helier* (Jersey, 1845).

   ,,   ,,   *Les États* (Jersey, 1847).

HAVET, *Les Cours Royales des Iles Normandes* (Paris, 1878).

   ,,   *Série Chronologique des Gardiens et Seigneurs des Iles Normandes*, included in the second volume of his *Opuscules Divers* (Paris, 1896).

SYVRET, *Chronique des Iles de Jersey, Guernesey, etc.* (Guernsey, 1832).

PAYNE, *An Armorial of Jersey* (Jersey, 1865).

TUPPER, *The History of Guernsey and its Bailiwick*, 2nd ed. (Guernsey, 1876).

   ,,   *The Chronicles of Castle Cornet* (Guernsey, 1851).

SINEL, *Prehistoric Times and Men of the Channel Islands* (Jersey, 1923).

Preface

Nicolle, *Mont Orgueil Castle* (Jersey, 1921).
Le Quesne, *A Constitutional History of Jersey* (London, 1856).

I have also derived much valuable information from the "Bulletins" and "Publications" of the Société Jersiaise (Jersey, 1873-1922), and from the "Transactions" of the Société Guernésiaise (Guernsey, 1883-1922). I also wish to acknowledge with sincere thanks the kindness I have received from several friends who have lent me rare books and family manuscripts, or have helped me with advice and suggestions.

The faults of omission and commission (of which nobody can be more painfully conscious than I am myself) may perhaps be explained by the fact that this revision was necessarily undertaken at a time when most of my books of reference were inaccessible and when I had innumerable other calls upon my time; and if that be not a sufficient excuse, I can only plead with the old writer that "who favlteth not, liueth not; who mendeth favlts is commended; the Printer hath favlted a little; it may be the avthor ouer-sighted more. Thy Paine (Reader) is the least; then erre not thov most by misconstrving or sharpe censvring; lest thov be more vncharitable than either of them hath been heedlesse."

E. F. C.

Guernsey.
November, 1923.

vii

CONTENTS

LIST OF ILLUSTRATIONS

ix

List of Illustrations

" Assurément quelques insulaires, isolés sur leurs rochers fertiles, pressés entre deux empires puissants souvent ennemis et toujours rivaux, qui pendant une longue suite de générations, et avec une fermeté inébranlable, ont défendu leurs institutions, leur nationalité et leur liberté, donnent un rare exemple qui peut faire réfléchir sur certaines théories contemporaines, et sur l'application qui en est décrétée pour le bonheur des peuples."—*Histoire du Cotentin et de ses Iles*, tome i., p. 99, par Gustave Dupont. (Caen, 1870.)

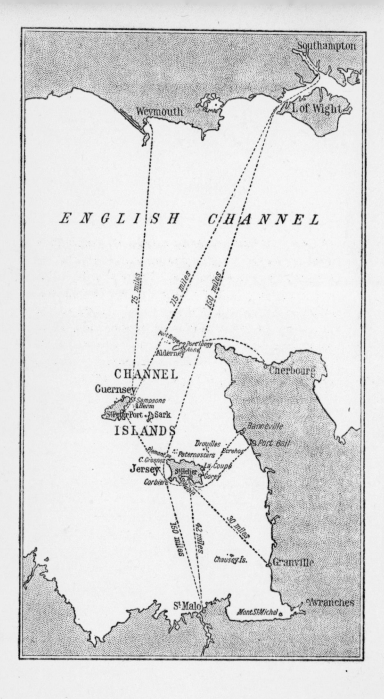

THE CHANNEL ISLANDS

CHAPTER I

IN THE BEGINNING

OFF the coast of the Cotentin, to the north of the Bay of Mont St. Michel, is to be found a group of islands, surrounded by islets, rocks, and reefs. These islands are called by the English the Channel Islands, by the French *Les Iles Normandes*. The group is composed of Jersey, Guernsey, Alderney, Sark, Herm, and Jethou, and a few minor rocks.

Jersey and Guernsey have each its own court and code of laws, and politically and socially their history is quite distinct. Alderney and Sark are included in the bailiwick of Guernsey. Herm and Jethou have no special administration, and are considered as detached portions of Guernsey territory.

The following pages will perhaps show that these islands, both historically and intrinsically, merit more attention than has generally been given to them.

That they are the oldest possessions of the British Crown is evident from the fact that they comprise the only territory remaining to England of the old Duchy of Normandy. The predecessor of our Sovereign was Duke of Normandy ere he was King of England, and as Duke he ruled that little archipelago off the Norman coast which, alone of all their once fair French provinces, has been retained by the monarchs who were so long styled the rulers of "Great Britain, France, and Ireland."

They helped under William to conquer England in the year 1066, and ever since have remained loyal to the English kings as representatives of their Norman dukes.

During the quaternary period a study of the strata on their sea-coasts proves that Jersey and Alderney were alternately attached and separated from the Continent no fewer than three times, although Guernsey, Sark, and Herm were only twice reconnected with the mainland, and thus were well out in the sea so much earlier than their neighbours that the moles, so prevalent on the other two islands, were unable to attain their shores.

But in all the Islands archæologists will find records of the past, tracing human succession from the earliest Palæolithic to the latest Neolithic times. In the two Mousterian land caves of Jersey—caves which were human habitations when the sea was still far away—remains have been found not only of the mammoth and Arctic lemming, the woolly rhinoceros, the reindeer and the great auk, but of the flint implements with which contemporary man both defended himself from his neighbours and provided his daily food. Indeed, human teeth, which have been identified as those of a Neanderthal man, have also been found imbedded behind the hearth of the cave of La Cotte, St. Brelade.[1]

[1] *Prehistoric Times and Men in the Channel Islands*, by Joseph Sinel, second edition, 1923.

In the Beginning

This era is replaced—how many thousand years later?—by the earliest Neolithic or Tardenoisian period, which is traceable beneath the levels of the submerged forest land and also by some tombs and human remains which have been found both in Jersey and Guernsey. In its turn this was succeeded by the later Neolithic period —a period which is now considered to have closed about 2000 B.C., and is abundantly represented by the menhirs and dolmens, "grey recumbent tombs of the dead in desert places" which abound throughout the Islands. While a specimen of the earliest type of the abode of the living, namely a hut circle—the first to be recorded in the Islands—consisting of an avenue of approach, pillared doorway, circular walls, paved floor, bed, hearth, and with urns dating from the Bronze Age imbedded in the soil, was excavated from a "tertre" or mound, in Jersey, in June, 1923.

Poingdestre, the Jersey historian, states that in his time (1609-91) there were in Jersey no fewer than 70 dolmens, while in Guernsey, Colonel de Guèrin[1] has traced from local "Livres de Perchage" (or "terriers" as they are called in England) the names of 68 dolmens and cists and 39 menhirs—of which, respectively, 15 and 6 still exist. These megaliths occur in groups including both dolmens and menhirs, and, curiously enough, there is a difference in type between those of the different islands, those of Jersey resembling those of

[1] "An Annotated List of Dolmens, Menhirs, etc.," compiled by Colonel T. W. M. de Guèrin (*Proceedings of the Société Guernésiaise*, 1921).

The Channel Islands

Le Cotentin, those of Guernsey being of the same type as those found in Lower Brittany. Yet they each partake of the tradition of sanctity—whether in true or inverted form—which has persisted almost to our own time, and in their neighbourhood lingers the feeling of trespass where the old gods still claim homage. For, as in Normandy and Brittany, the local association between great stone monuments and primitive magic and religion is a very strong one. Indeed, there is reason to believe that witchcraft is but a survival of the ancient worship of the sun and moon, of the great forces of nature, embodying the enormous concern of primitive mankind for the increase of their flocks and herds and of their belief in the influence of sex on vegetable fertility. This resulted in orgiastic festivals during seed-time and harvest, in the worship of Ishtar and of Ashtoreth, of Diana, and of Venus, of the gods of the sacred tree, the sacred stone, the holy well, of the goddesses of night and the underworld, which has persisted even down to our own times as witchcraft among the uneducated, as Satanism among the adepts. Indeed, the Earth-mother, "goddess of many names, in every clime adored," is represented in Guernsey by the two statue-menhirs standing outside the Churches of St. Mary de Castro and St. Martin respectively, and by the rudely sculptured figure on the underside of the capstone of the great Déhus dolmen. Moreover, not only does the orientation of the dolmens in all the islands, as well as certain mystic signs on some of the stones in Brittany, imply the influence of the sun, moon, and stars, but

In the Beginning

local tradition has identified the Roque Berg in Jersey and the Catioroc in Guernsey as the site of the insular Witches' "Sabbats."

In connection with the prevalence of witchcraft even to this day in the Channel Islands, it is important to note that the Eddic poems called the Helgi Lays, which Dr. Vigfusson has shown to refer, among other localities, to Guernsey, mention Gaulish sibyls who were thus described by Pomponius Mela : " Priestesses, living in the holiness of perpetual virginity and . . . believed to be endowed with extraordinary gifts, namely to rouse the sea and wind by their incantations, to turn themselves into whatever animal form they may choose, to cure disease, to know what is to come and to foretell it." And in one of these lays one of the characters taunts another in words which have been rendered as follows :

> " Thou wert a sibyl in Guernsey,
> Deceitful hag, setting lies together."[1]

---

[1] *Lectures on Celtic Heathendom*, p. 198, by Sir John Rhys. (London, 1888.)

CHAPTER II

THE DAWN OF CIVILISATION

In process of time the Stone Age was superseded by that of Bronze, of which various relics—principally found in Alderney—consisting of socketed axe-heads, swords, spears, etc., are to be seen in the local museums. But far the most important survivals of this period are the hut circle found in Jersey in 1923, and the gold torque—possibly of Irish origin—found in 1889, some three feet below the surface of a site in St. Helier, as also certain Gaulish coins, found in all the Islands and actually minted in the Islands themselves, of a type prevalent, more particularly, among the *Unelli* who were then known to be established in the Cotentin.[1] We next come to the evidences of the Roman occupation of the Islands.

Jersey and Guernsey are supposed to owe their traditional names of Caesarea and Sarnia respectively to these conquerors; and, from a nearly perfect series of Roman coins unearthed at different periods in Jersey, Guernsey, Alderney, and Sark, it is evident that there was at least a constant intercourse between their inhabitants and Italy from the reign of Caligula to that

[1] *Proceedings of British Numismatic Society*, 1913, and article by Father A. Bourde de la Rogerie in *Proceedings of Société Guernésiaise*, 1922.

7

The Channel Islands

of Honorius. An interesting confirmation of this intercourse was revealed in 1916, when Monsieur Allegrini of Corsica dug up in his garden a bronze plaque dated A.D. 71, commemorating the donation of the citizenship of Rome to Basiel, son of Turbel, " Gallinaria *Sarniensis*," for his twenty-six years' good service in the fleet of the Emperor Vespasian.[1] Thus Basiel leaps into fame as being the first Channel Islander recorded in history. He was, probably, one of the aboriginal Celts whose descendants were, in the seventh and eighth centuries A.D., overwhelmed by a people who, though they eventually adopted the French tongue, did not become a part of the French State. That people, Normans of Scandinavian descent, brought England by force of arms under their own dukes. In continental Normandy, language and geography made them Frenchmen; in the Islands, political traditions and inherent loyalty prevailed against language and geography. Therefore the Channel Islander never became a Frenchman, though neither did he become an Englishman, but he alone remained Norman, keeping his own language, his own customs, and his own laws, independent of the English Parliament, but attached to the English Crown.

In the first few centuries of our era there was a perpetual interchange of men and ideas between Brittany and Normandy on the one hand, and Ireland and Great Britain on the other. Almost all the early Bas Breton "saints" (as these missionaries were generally termed)

[1] *Bulletin de la Société des Sciences Historiques, etc., de la Corse*, 1921, pp. 57-66.

The Dawn of Civilisation

were either born or brought up in Ireland, Cornwall, or Wales, and they must indeed have had great courage and devotion to trust themselves, as they did, upon the stormy waters of the Channel in the frail barks of that period.

The first of these missionaries to visit the Islands was St. Marcouf, who came to Jersey in 540, and was so successful that he established a religious community in the northern part of the island, probably on the site afterwards occupied by the priory of Bonne Nuit. He was succeeded by St. Sampson, who, after being educated in Glamorgan by St. Iltut, was driven out of England by the Saxons and took refuge in Normandy, where he was made Bishop of Dol, his diocese including the islands of Jersey, Guernsey, and Sark, although Dr. Fawteir, his latest biographer, denies that he ever was a bishop.[1]

According to tradition, St. Sampson embarked for Guernsey, and having landed at the harbour which still bears his name, he there caused a chapel or oratory to be built, and established a chaplain and other priests to carry on the work he had begun. But all that can historically be vouched for is that he and Duke Jual of Brittany visited the islands of Lesia and Augia— islands which were identified some six to seven centuries later by monkish chroniclers as Guernsey and Jersey.

In the meantime the remaining portion of Jersey was being converted by St. Helier, a disciple of St. Marcouf.

[1] *Annales de Bretagne*, xxxv., No. 2.

The Channel Islands

He started his mission in Jersey in 555, and there built a hermitage upon a rock, which in those days was surrounded by marshes and meadows, all of them now submerged and forming part of St. Aubin's Bay. But in 559 he was massacred by the chieftain of a horde of Saxon or Danish pirates who invaded the island, and thus he became Jersey's first Christian martyr.

In Mr. Poingdestre's manuscript in the British Museum[1] this hermitage is thus described: "There is a little Islet, or rather a Rock, at Bowshot distance from ye New-Castle,[2] more into the sea, called St. Helerye's Island, in ye fashion of an Ermitage where his cell remains to this day, hewen into the rock, with a Couch of the same rock, where he is sayd to have passed his dayes in great hardship; which Cell hath been in times pass't much frequented by pilgrims from farre and neere upon ye score of devotion.

"Sir Thomas Morgan in his last yeere did cause that Rocke to be fortifyed and planted ordinance upon it. The Towne Church and Parish are dedicated to this Saint and beare his name; and soe did ye Church and Abbey which was built in ye place where nowe is ye Lower Guard of Elizabeth Castle, which Church was muche commended for goodnesse of structure; and ye quire of it remained entire till ye siedge of 1651 by Colonell Haines, when it was quite ruined by ye fall of a Bombe through the roofe of it downe to a roome whiche had been made under it full of powder, which

---

[1] Harleian MSS. No. 5417.
[2] Elizabeth Castle.

tooke and blewe it up, and with it neere foure score men." [1]

In close vicinity to this hermitage, the Abbey of St. Helier was founded, about the middle of the twelfth century, by Guillaume FitzHamon, a rich Norman seigneur. This Abbey was affiliated to the Abbey of Notre Dame du Vœu at Cherbourg in 1184, and appropriated to the Crown by Henry VIII.; it was demolished and the fortifications of Elizabeth Castle were begun in the year 1551. To help towards the payment of this new fortress the bells in every church, one excepted, were taken down and sold, realising the sum of £171 9s. [2] But the ship which was conveying these bells to France foundered in the harbour, and everything was lost, which showed the wrath of Heaven at this sacrilege. "Since then, before a storm these bells always ring up from the deep; and to this day the fishermen of St. Ouen's Bay always go to the edge of the water before embarking, to listen if they can 'hear the bells upon the wind,' and if those warning notes are heard, nothing will induce them to leave the shore." [3]

But we have wandered from our patron saints.

St. Sampson was succeeded by his nephew, St. Magloire. According to tradition St. Magloire had been given the greatest part of the island of Sark by a Count Loyescon—one of the Armorican chieftains who

---

[1] Printed in the 10me *Bulletin of the Société Jersiaise.*

[2] *Jersey, ses Antiquités,* by De la Croix, t. i., p. 219.

[3] *Notes and Queries,* First Series, vol. xi. (April 7, 1885).

in those days were successively owners of the Islands—in gratitude for a miraculous cure which the saint had wrought. So to Sark St. Magloire repaired, and there he founded a monastery and a school, to which youths were sent from Normandy, Brittany, and even Great Britain.

At this time Guernsey was owned by a chief called Nivo, who, hearing of St. Magloire's fame, asked him to come over and cure his daughter, who was dumb. St. Magloire performed this miracle, and in return Nivo granted him a third of Guernsey. This induced St. Magloire to come to the island and build a chapel in the Vale parish which has long ago fallen into ruins; and he also founded chapels in Jersey and Herm. He then went back to his monastery in Sark, where he died.

Other early "saints" came and went between Britain and the Islands—St. Paterne, St. Aubin, and St. Brelade, who has been identified with the Irish saint Brandon. Pretextat, Archbishop of Rouen, who had incurred the wrath of Fredegonde, wife of King Chilperic, was exiled to Jersey, and undoubtedly the presence of an Archbishop of the Church must have materially assisted the process of conversion in the Islands, though it is to St. Marcouf, St. Helier, and St. Magloire that we are principally indebted for the blessings of Christianity and civilisation.

But the years to come did not bring peace. Hordes of wild pirates from the far north came down upon the Islands time after time, burning, pillaging and conquering. As Wace, the historian-poet of Jersey says:

ST. AUBIN, JERSEY.

The Dawn of Civilisation

" De sa gent è de sa contrée
En plusieurs liex part la ruine
Ke firent la gent Sarrazine
En Aureni, en Guernesi,
En Saire, en Erin, en Gersi."[1]

It is noticeable that Wace speaks of these tribes of barbarians as " la gent *Sarrazine*"; the old French word " Sarrazin" implying any foreigner or alien who need not necessarily be of Eastern origin.

Thus the *hougue* in Guernsey, now covered by the Castel Church, was called by the Islanders the Chastel du Grand Geffroy or du Grand Sarrazin, and from this castle the parish takes its name of Ste. Marie de Castro. This " Grand Geffroy" was undoubtedly the celebrated Jarl, Godefroy, son of Harold. His personality must have deeply impressed the Islanders, one of the dolmens in the Vale parish being known as the Tombeau du Grand Sarrazin. Hastings, another well-known Jarl, gave his name to the Hougue Hatenaie, which is the highest ground in the parish of St. Martin.

These Scandinavians have left an enduring token of their presence in the names they gave to different places : thus the Norse *o* or *ey*, an island, appears in Jers*ey*, Guern*sey*, Alder*ney*; and *holme*, a river island, in Li*hou*, Jet*hou*, Bur*hou*, etc.[2]

They also have left us as legacies the *hougues*, or artificial mounds of earth which they raised over their dead chieftains.

[1] *Roman de Rou*, t. i., p. 21. It is easy to recognise the names of Alderney, Guernsey, Sark, Herm, and Jersey.
[2] *Words and Places*, by Isaac Taylor, pp. 124-5.

The Channel Islands

In Jersey the principal *hougue* is the Hougue Bie or Hougue Bie de Hambie, to which one of the most widely known of the insular legends is attached. Perhaps the earliest extant account of it is in *Les Chroniques de Jersey*, printed in Guernsey in 1832 from a manuscript written in 1585 belonging to the de Carteret family, which may be roughly translated thus:

Once upon a time in the island of Jersey there was a serpent who with many griefs and pains troubled the Islanders. The Seigneur de Hambie in Normandy having heard of it, and wishing to acquire fame and to make his name glorious for ever, came over to Jersey, killed the serpent, and cut off its head. But the varlet who accompanied him, wishing to take unto himself the glory of this action, and being mad with envy, contrived to kill his master and bury him. He then returned to Hambie and persuaded Madame de Hambie that the serpent had killed his lord, but that he had avenged the death of his master by killing the serpent. He also persuaded her that his master's dying wish was that she should espouse him, which she did, but only for the love of her late lord. But the servant, having become master, was troubled in his sleep, and nervous, and cried out in the night, "Oh, miserable that I am, who have killed my master!" The lady often warned him of these dreams, but as they still continued, she began to suspect him of this parricide, and told her friends, and the servant having been examined, by the decree of the judge was found guilty. In memory of this event, the lady raised a monument upon the spot where she learned her husband had been killed and buried. This monument was a round tower on an elevated spot, which place is called La Hougue Bie, and from it can be seen in clear weather the castle and hamlet of Hambie in Normandy.

The author of the *Chroniques* goes on to say " Sire [1] Richard Mabon, priest and vicar of the parish of St. Martin and afterwards dean of the island of Jersey under the Bishop of Coutances, having been to Jerusalem, on his return from the said journey caused a chapel to be built on the summit of this *hougue*, which chapel he named Notre Dame de la Hougue Bie, because he built it on this *hougue* in perpetual memory of the Holy Sepulchre." This chapel was superimposed upon a twelfth-century foundation, and he developed a peculiar reverence for the place by encouraging the idea that the Virgin Mary frequently appeared there to him; and he placed her figure in an excavation underground, formed to resemble the Holy Sepulchre at Jerusalem, and entered by a vaulted passage, through which the people passed to pay their devotions. At the middle of this passage the figure was seen through

---

[1] In the Channel Islands, up to the Reformation, all ecclesiastics under the rank of dean were invariably styled "sire," probably as the French equivalent of the Latin *dominus*, by which term they were known in the more ancient deeds. The practice must have been the same in England, for in Shakespeare's *Love's Labour's Lost* we find the curate is called " Sir Nathaniel," and "Sir Oliver Martext" is the Vicar in *As You Like It;* this prefix indicating that the priest, though not a University man, was ordained.

an opening, leaning on one elbow with a hand extended to receive the gifts which all who visited the chapel were expected to present. When the novelty of this spectacle wore off and visitors began to slacken, he announced that the Virgin would for the future perform many miracles at the *hougue*, and by a system of artificial lights and concealed wires produced a series of manifestations which impressed numbers of the people; but eventually much of his trickery was discovered, and gave rise to the expression that anything very incredible was a " Miracle de la Hougue Bie." [1]

At the beginning of the nineteenth century this spot was converted into a naval lookout and summer residence by Admiral Philip d'Auvergne, Duc de Bouillon, it having been transferred to him in 1792 by his uncle, General James d'Auvergne, who "with questionable taste incorporated this interesting structure with a tower, which he built on its site, and which is generally called, from its later owner, Prince's Tower." [2] This monument has now been taken over by the Société Jersiaise, who are removing all the modern additions, and are bringing to light whatever may remain of the old chapels. They also hope to discover the (probable) megalithic remains over which the tumulus was originally erected.

In 933 Raoul, King of the Franks, ceded to William Longsword, second Duke of Normandy, the land

---

[1] MSS. of Thomas le Maistre, quoted by Durell in his edition of Falle's *History of Jersey*.

[2] *Armorial of Jersey*, by Bertrand Payne, vol. i., p. 58.

BELCROUTE BAY, JERSEY.

situated, as Dupont describes it, "on the sea coasts of the Bretons."[1]

As we have seen, the Islands had been previously held by a succession of Breton chieftains such as Loyescon and Nivo, and then by northern Jarls such as "le Grand Sarrazin," but this charter definitely incorporated them with Normandy and placed them under the dominion of the Norman dukes.

Mauger, uncle of William the Conqueror and Archbishop of Rouen, was banished to Guernsey in 1055, and many legends concerning him still exist. One is that he landed at La "Baie de Sains" or "de Seing," a name now modernised into "Saints" Bay, and that there he fell in love with a fair country girl[2] called Gille (of whose kindred the insular family of Guille claim to be), and that from them descended the family of Mauger of Guernsey, Jersey and Sark.

Of course, it is impossible to verify this tradition, but it appears from the earliest known legal documents that the families of Guille and Mauger have held land in St. Martin's parish in the "Contrée de Seing" certainly since the year 1303, the earliest date to which our information goes back.

Mauger, who was noted for his crimes, is also credited with having introduced witchcraft and sorcery into the island.

Less than a century later, about the year 1120, the

---

[1] *Le Cotentin et ses Iles*, t. i., p. 156.

[2] An old manuscript quoted in the *Chronique de Normandie*, Rouen, 1578, folio 79, calls her a " noble dame."

poet Wace was born in Jersey. He was partly educated at Caen, and died in England about 1184. A tablet dedicated to his memory was unveiled in the Royal Square, Jersey, in May, 1923. Two of the most celebrated of his poems are *Brut*, which is a collection of all the legends extant in Brittany, and apparently in the Islands, about King Arthur, his Court, and the Knights of the Holy Grail; and the *Roman de Rou*, which contains an account of the first incursions of the Northmen into England and France and the history of Rollo and his successors down to 1106. They are the most curious literary monuments that remain of the history, language and traditions of ducal Normandy. Their vernacular, with very little alteration, is the dialect still spoken in the country parishes of all the Islands, and they are specimens of the Norman-French which was for centuries the legal language of England, and in which even now the Royal assent to any Bill is given, reminding every Briton that he still owes allegiance to the Duke of Normandy, and that the language which claims precedence in his history is not English but French.[1]

With the thirteenth century a new era began for the Islands. In 1199, John, who as Comte de Mortain, had held these Islands in fief for the past twelve months, succeeded to the throne of England and the dukedom

[1] French predominated at the English Court. If the first three Edwards understood English, which is doubtful, they made scanty use of it. Henry IV. (1399-1413) seems to have been the first King after the Conquest who addressed a speech in English to his Parliament. It was not until 1731 that the records of law-suits in England were transcribed in English instead of French or Latin.

The Dawn of Civilisation

of Normandy, and he soon realised that his Norman subjects were among the most difficult problems with which he had to deal.

The family of de Préaux was then one of the most distinguished in Upper Normandy. Wace mentions a seigneur of this name among the combatants at Hastings;[1] and William de Préaux, one of his descendants, accompanied Richard Cœur de Lion to the Crusades, and there saved his life at the risk of his own.[2] King John, knowing that the barons of the Cotentin were wavering in their allegiance, wished to establish in this part of his duchy a man on whose fidelity he could rely. By a charter dated January 4, 1200, he nominated Pierre de Préaux Seigneur (dominus)[3] of Jersey, Guernsey, Alderney and the dependencies, at the same time giving him other lands both in England and in Normandy, all of which he held from the King by the feudal service of three knights,[4] and he also received the promise of succeeding William de Vernon (whose eldest daughter, Marie, he had married)[5] in the lordship of the Isle of Wight.

The seal of this Pierre de Préaux forms part of the Collection Sphragistique des Archives Nationales de France.[6] It shows the arms that the Priaulx family of Guernsey bear to this day—an eagle displayed—and

[1] *Roman de Rou*, t. ii., p. 248, n. 2.
[2] Dupont, t. i., p. 524.
[3] *Ibid.*, pp. 425 and 489.
[4] Rot. Chart, p. 33, col. 2, and p. 71, col. 1.
[5] *Jersey, ses Antiquités*, t. i., p. 154.
[6] No. 3305.

around the seal is the legend *Sigillum Petri de Pratellis*.[1]

Thus were the Islands, for the first time since the sixth century, united under a single ruler and politically separated from the Cotentin. The gift of the Islands to Pierre de Préaux seems to have been practically absolute, for by a still extant charter he gave the islets of Ecrehou in 1203 to the abbey of Val Richer for the purpose of constructing a chapel dedicated to God and the Virgin, where Masses were to be said for the souls of the founder, of his ancestors, and for the King of England. But, in 1204, Pierre de Préaux, who, unlike most of his contemporaries, had hitherto remained faithful to King John—despite the fact that Philip Augustus of France was busily conquering Normandy and confiscating all the Norman fiefs belonging to English partisans—was also made Governor of Rouen. Rouen was then strenuously holding out against the French, and was the last hope of the English in Normandy. As a last resort Philip Augustus offered Pierre a large bribe of land and titles if he would surrender the town. "Every man has his price" and Pierre succumbed. But, when he claimed the fulfilment of the French King's promise, Philip Augustus cynically inserted the condition that on the deed of gift it should be explained that this was the price paid for the surrender of Rouen. These words changed the destiny of the Channel Islands, for de Préaux—too late, alas! for

[1] The Latin form of de Préaux. See *Gardiens et Seigneurs des Iles Normandes*, by J. Havet, pp. 385-6.

his reputation—repudiated this invidious grant, and, having wrested a reluctant pardon from King John, retained his lordship of the Channel Islands. The result being that, in the final treaty between France and England which he helped to frame, in the list of the Norman possessions abandoned by King John to France, the Channel Islands were not included.[1]

Thus originally all the Islands were administered by one man, uniting in himself both civil and military power, presiding over the "Royal Courts" of Jersey and Guernsey, and being styled indifferently "Governor" or "Bailiff."

Towards the year 1290 Otho de Grandison, then Governor of the Islands, delegated the civil power to two subordinate officers, known as "bailiffs": and since then Jersey and Guernsey have each had its bailiff, and the Governorship resolved itself into the military command. From the middle of the fifteenth century the Islands were definitely divided into two governments, Jersey being one, and Guernsey with the lesser islands the other. Since 1835 in Guernsey, and 1854 in Jersey, only Lieutenant-Governors have been appointed, and the office of Governor is in abeyance.

The possession of these Islands was ratified to the Crown of England by the treaty of 1259, by which the King of England recognised that he held them of the King of France in fief, owing homage for the same,

---

[1] Dupont, t. i., pp. 455-9 ; and *Memoires de la Soc. des Antiquaires de l'Ouest*, t. 12 : article on "Jean Sans-Terre," by M. le Cointre Dupont, p. 193.

until the treaty of Bretigny in 1360, by which the King of France abandoned this right of suzerainty. Although until the year 1568 the Islands were still so far united to Normandy that they remained included within the diocese of Coutances, their inhabitants were now no longer vassals of France, but subjects of England, and had started a distinct political career, having for its basis the defence of their nationality against France and of their independence against England.

CHAPTER III

FIEFS AND FEUDAL TENURES

BEFORE we proceed to touch upon the individual history of the Channel Islands, it may be worth while to notice the feudal system of Jersey and Guernsey, the history of some of the principal fiefs, their quaint tenures and their manorial courts. For fragments of the old system remain to this day, and may almost be said to constitute one of the peculiar charms of the Islands, though most people from want of knowledge fail to recognise these picturesque survivals of mediæval customs.

By the time of the Norman Conquest the feudal system was in full force in the Islands, and society consisted of those who fought, those who prayed, and those who laboured—*i.e.*, the nobles, the clergy, and the peasants. Here, as elsewhere, the fiefs were divided into two classes—the " fief haubert," for which homage was owed to the King in person and the Seigneur, whilst protecting his vassals, owed military service to the Crown; and the "fief subalterne," or minor fief, whose seigneur had less important duties to perform and owed homage merely to an over-lord, of whose seigneurie his fief was a dependency. But the general fact emerges that among the Channel Islanders —as among all other descendants of the Northmen—

there was less distinction of class than among the English of that period; that among them the tiller of the soil was still an efficient warrior, and that the broad distinction between the lord and his serf was not the important thing it already was among the Saxons. For the Viking was a merchant as well as a fighter, therefore to him the progress "from status to contract" came naturally.

In the Islands, strictly speaking, St. Ouen alone can claim the distinction of being a "fief haubert," for, never having escheated into the King's hands, it alone retains its original tenure. Although modified by modern usage, it originally comprised homage, knight's service rendered to the King in the "Château de Gourroic" (now called "Mont Orgueil") at the Seigneur's own expense, and also providing two horsemen duly armed and caparisoned; "garde noble," and with rights of "haute, moyenne et basse justice," implying that the Seigneur could condemn any of his vassals to be hanged, imprisoned, or simply beaten with rods; while, in 1607, before the Royal Commissioners the then Seigneur of St. Ouen successfully established his claim to "keep his court" within the ruined castle of Grosnez, as his ancestors had done from time immemorial. But Rosel, Samarès, Trinity, and, since the days of Charles II., Mélesches, are held "in capite" from the King and owe "suite de cour," that is, attendance at the "Assise d'Héritage" (or "Chief Pleas," as the corresponding sessions of the Royal Court are called in Guernsey), knight service, and "relief" whenever the heir of the manor comes into his inheritance. To seek the origin of the presence of the Seigneurs at the Royal Courts, we must go back to a remote period before the constitutions of King John. Feudal tenure always implied the duty and the right of jurisdiction of some kind, therefore the Seigneurs attended as judges and not as vassals.

According to the Extent of 1331, Sir Reginald de Carteret was then Seigneur of St. Ouen, and, as the author of the *Chroniques de Jersey* expresses it, his ancestors had held that fief "tant du Roy d'Angleterre que des Ducs de Normandie qu'il n'y en avoit mémoire du contraire." These de Carterets are, indeed, the oldest and most distinguished family in the Channel Islands. For nearly a thousand years they have been the principal landowners, if not virtual rulers,[1] of Jersey; they were granted Sark by Queen Elizabeth in 1565,[2] and Alderney by Charles II. in 1660.

Humphrey and Mauger de Carteret accompanied Duke William to England and fought at Hastings; Sir Reginald de Carteret, Seigneur of St. Ouen, went to the Crusades, and was present at the taking of Jerusalem.

On July 24, 1203, Pierre de Préaux received orders from King John to raise an aid from the seigneurs and vassals of the different fiefs for the payment of the men

[1] "From 1626 to 1826, with but nine years' cessation during the Protectorate, the family of de Carteret had held the office of Bailly of Jersey" (*Armorial*, p. 117).

[2] "In Reward of the many services received by Herself and Her Royal Ancestors from this family" (Patent of Queen Elizabeth to Helier de Carteret).

employed in their defence, which order implies that the King preferred to receive a money payment (or "aid") for the payment of mercenaries instead of personal service, and to Reginald de Carteret was given the charge of receiving this "aid."

At the time of the separation from Normandy the de Carterets were among the few Norman lords who, putting duty and honour above interest, adhered to their English King, and thereby forfeited their far more valuable lands and lordships on the Continent.

Before 1234 [1] Sir Philip de Carteret, grandson of the above-named Reginald, married Margaret d'Albini, niece of the celebrated Philip d'Albini, twice Governor of these Islands; and from them sprang seven generations of de Carterets, who fought and defeated the French and served their country with honour and distinction until the days of Philip de Carteret, the eighth of that name. His father having died in his infancy, this Philip was for eighteen years a ward of the Crown, and an ancient manuscript records that when he came of age alder-trees were growing in the hall of his manor-house of St. Ouen, owing to the neglect and covetousness of his guardians. By his bold remonstrances against the abuse of power exercised by Matthew Baker the Governor, and the exorbitant taxes which he levied on the people, Philip incurred the resentment of that official. In revenge Baker tried to implicate him in the guilt of his father-in-law; for Philip had married Margaret, daughter of Richard Harliston, an ardent

---

[1] Extent of Jersey, 1248.

Fiefs and Feudal Tenures

Yorkist, who had been made, for his services to Edward IV., the Yorkist King, Governor of Jersey. After Edward's death Harliston, deposed from his command in Jersey, joined the Court of the Duchess of Burgundy, in later years an adherent of Perkin Warbeck, the pretender who falsely claimed to be Edward's son.[1] Baker therefore suborned a menial named Roger le Bouteillier —a man discharged by de Carteret for forgery and theft of his signet ring—to write a letter, purporting to be written by his late master, in which he offered to betray Jersey to France. This letter Roger le Bouteillier pretended to pick up in the road, after the Seigneur of St. Ouen and his retinue had passed *en route* to the "Cohue" (or Royal Court), and handed to Matthew Baker, bound for the same place from his residence at Mont Orgueil. Matthew rode straightway to the Court, where he proclaimed Philip de Carteret a traitor. The Bailiff, Clement le Hardy, took Baker's part, for, having been appointed by the Governor, he felt his tenure of office depended on keeping in his favour, and he also had a private grudge against Madame de St. Ouen, in that she had addressed him one day as " Gossip " *(compère)* instead of calling him " Monsieur de Bailly."[2] So he ordered Philip to be led off to the dungeon of Mont Orgueil and his estate to be confiscated, without going through the formality of a trial. At this fresh insult Philip threw down his glove, and challenged to mortal combat any man who should dare affirm that he was

[1] Le Quesne's *Constitutional History of Jersey,* pp. 125-6.
[2] *Chroniques,* p. 35.

the writer of the letter. Roger le Bouteillier was the only man who took up the challenge, and him—a low-born felon—Philip was reluctant to fight. But both the Governor and the Bailiff insisted that this acceptance was valid. Philip was led away to a loathsome dungeon, where he was deliberately kept in a half-starved condition, while le Bouteillier, nominally a prisoner, went and came as he liked, and was "bien nourri pour être fort," as the old chronicler puts it.

Meanwhile the lists for this unequal "combat à outrance" were prepared on Grouville Common, and the date was fixed for the eve of St. Lawrence's Day, August 9, 1494—about a fortnight after the pretended discovery of the letter.

These arrangements having been made, Baker hurried off to England to tell his story to the King, having first issued a proclamation by the Vicomte that no boats or vessels should quit the island without a special licence from himself, so afraid was he of being forestalled. Now Madame de St. Ouen was lying with her four-day-old son on her arm wondering why her husband did not return. When at last she heard what had happened, the chronicle states, "elle prinst courage et, se confiant totallement en Dieu," determined to do all she could to save her husband. She got out of bed, and, with only one attendant, managed to slip out of Jersey in an open boat at dead of night and attain the neighbouring island of Guernsey. On arrival she went to the house of William de Beauvoir, a jurat of the Royal Court, sometime (through his mother, Margaret le Feyvre, daughter of Michel le Feyvre) Seigneur of Vinchelés-de-Bas in Jersey, and an old and trusted friend of the de Carterets.

He, being a man of courage and decision, immediately started with her in his own boat to Poole. Through great peril they arrived at Poole Harbour, but what was their dismay at seeing Matthew Baker standing on the quay! They would now have been discovered if a hail-storm had not come on, "comme Dieu voulut, ayant toujours soin des siens," of so violent a character that Baker was glad to seek shelter in a shed, and to remain there while the lady landed in safety and was hospitably received by James Haviland, then Mayor of Poole, husband of Helène, daughter of Richard de Beauvoir, of Guernsey.

At break of day Madame de St. Ouen and her faithful friend set off on horseback and rode to Winchester, where the King was holding his Court. On arrival she went straight to an old friend of her husband's, Thomas Langton, Bishop of Winchester, and by his means obtained a personal audience of King Henry VII. Being, like all the Tudors, partial to a pretty woman, and struck by her courage and endurance, Henry gave her a royal warrant under the Great Seal of England for the deliverance of her husband. Fate so willed it that, as she came down the stairs from the audience chamber, she met Baker ascending them, and great was his astonishment and fury at seeing her there and feeling that he had been foiled.

Fortune still favouring her, she arrived in Jersey on

August 8, the day before the date fixed for the combat. She went straight to the Bailiff's house, and, displaying her warrant, demanded her husband's immediate release, and that he should be at once restored to his dignities and honours. Then was there great joy amongst the people, for he was much beloved, "et n'y avoit personne qui ne priast Dieu pour luy."

On the following day, when the now useless lists came to be destroyed, it was discovered that the arena was studded with numerous and deep pits, which, carefully covered over with grass and known to and avoided by his adversary, would have rendered the death of the seigneur all but certain.

For his share in this disgraceful transaction Matthew Baker was deprived of his post, and Henry VII. at the same time issued an order that every loyal Islander should be allowed to come and go between England and the other Islands without asking leave of the Governor.

Philip de Carteret lived until August 1500; he and his wife are said to have had twenty sons, all distinguished for their prowess, and one daughter, Mabel, who married Drouet Lemprière, Seigneur of Trinity. From Edward, the eldest son, came the Carterets, knights, baronets and earls, whose most famous representative John Lord Carteret, eventually, in right of his mother, Earl Granville, was, at several times, Lord of the Bed Chamber, Secretary of State, Lord Lieutenant of Ireland, Knight of the Garter, and President of the Council.[1] Of him Horace Walpole said that in all his

---

[1] Le Quesne's *Constitutional History of Jersey*, pp. 125-6.

life he had only seen five great men, "and the greatest genius of the five was Carteret."[1] The title became extinct in 1775 by the death of Robert, second Earl Granville, Viscount Carteret, and the last Seigneur of St. Ouen in the male line. This historic fief then passed to his kinswoman, Jane Dumaresq, wife of Elias le Maistre, who thus became lady of the manor, and her great-great-grandson, Reginald Malet de Carteret, is the twenty-eighth Seigneur of St. Ouen,[2] and represents the ancient family of Malet, Seigneurs of La Malletière from A.D. 1180, as well as the senior branch of de Carteret.

There is no other house in the Islands to approach in beauty, size, or interest the old manor-house of St. Ouen. It has, of course, been added to and rebuilt at different periods, but its moat, Norman keep, and old arched doorways go back to the period of the early Plantagenets. The Seigneur of St. Ouen has no title-deeds; since the date when the Norman duke first granted this domain to his ancestor, it has always remained in the de Carteret family, so that no deeds of sale or purchase are in existence.

The next fief in seniority is that of Rosel. Before the alienation of Normandy, the Manor of Rosel was held by Sylvester de Furnet, who proved to be disloyal to King John, and his lands were confiscated and given to his brother Enguerrand in 1208. In 1228 the King granted these lands to Emery Buche, of Jersey, and they

[1] *Lord Carteret, a Political Biography*, by Archibald Ballantyne, p. ix.

[2] *The Ancestor* for October, 1902, pp. 218-222.

were transferred by the King in 1247 to Dreux de Barentin for "so long as the lands of England and Normandy are not united." [1]

In the oft-quoted Extent of 1331 we find William de Barentin, nephew and heir of Sir Drouet de Barentin, knight, holds the manor and fief of Rosel by "homage and relief," and "should our lord the King land in this island, the said William is bound to go on horseback into the sea to meet him, until the sea shall touch the girths of his horse, and in the same manner should attend him on his departure." [2]

He also owed "suite de cour," with the additional right of being Cup-bearer to the King during any stay the latter might make in the island. In July 1921, when His Majesty with the Queen and Princess Mary visited the Islands, these official duties were carried out by the present Seigneur of Rosel, Mr. R. R. Lemprière, who met the King on the pier (it being impossible with the present harbour accommodation to ride out into the sea), and was privileged to give the Royal party tea and refreshments at Mont Orgueil Castle—that being the sort of "Cup" His Majesty preferred. Mr. Lemprière was also considered to be a member of the Royal suite during the visit.

Philip de Barentin, who succeeded his father as seigneur, was accused by his relations of being a leper, and they made this a pretext for endeavouring to deprive

---

[1] *Lettres Closes*, published by the Société Jersiaise.

[2] The Fief des Augrès in Trinity parish was also held by the same tenure.

ST. OUEN MANOR, JERSEY.

him of his property. To frustrate these intentions, however, Philip made a hasty sale of his lands, Rosel, Samarès, and other manors, to Raoul Lemprière and Guillaume Payn in 1367, "conjointment"; in 1382 Payn and Lemprière divided these fiefs between themselves, Lemprière keeping Rosel and Payn taking Samarès, etc.

Being a leper, he had, of course, to separate from his wife and two sons, who remained at the manor pending a law-suit as to the legality of the sale. Scandal began to spread as to Madame de Barentin's too great familiarity with Jehannet de St. Martin, seigneur of the neighbouring manor of Trinity. What foundation this rumour had in fact, we shall never know, but it came to her ears, and she, according to the old manuscript,[1] thus addressed her two sons: "O, my sons, Jean de St. Martin has accused me of compromising myself with him. If you be loyal sons, you will avenge the insult offered to your mother. Such slanderers should have their tongues torn out." Then did Philip and Gilbert de Barentin lay an ambuscade along the road which led from their manor to that of Trinity, and posted a boy to warn them of the approach of M. de St. Martin, and as he unconsciously walked past, they leapt upon him, stabbed him to death with their poignards, and tore out his tongue by the roots.

What became of Madame de Barentin, thus taken at her word, history does not relate, but the murderers fled

[1] A sixteenth-century MS. quoted in the 27me *Bulletin of the Société Jersiaise*, p. 85.

to the nearest church, where alone they felt safe. In those days a church was a haven of refuge for malefactors; while inside its boundaries no one could touch them, but it could not grant them permanent immunity for their crimes. They could stay there for nine days without being molested, and their relations were allowed to bring them food, but they were under strict surveillance, and were then obliged to take an oath of abjuration of their country for ever. From each church the "grand chemin royal" ran to the seashore; it was known in Jersey by the name of "Perquage." [1] The rector of the parish, under whose protection they were, accompanied them to the seashore, seeing that they did not stray from the appointed route, for the slightest deviation would again put them in the power of the civil law. [2]

On the spot where this crime had been committed, a stone cross, called La Croix de Jehannet, was afterwards erected, and though this monument has long since disappeared, the district is still known as La Croix au Maître.

The present manor-house of Rosel is a modern building; the old house lay in the hollow below the present building, between the chapel and the Colombier; it must have existed even previous to 1200.

[1] A word derived from *perche*, a lineal measure 24 feet wide, the legal width of the Norman road.

[2] These "Perquages" were confiscated by the Crown at the Restoration. Charles II. gave them, May 30, 1663, to Sir Edward de Carteret, son of Sir Philip, who left no descendants, and they were inherited by his cousin, Anne Brevint, wife of the Dean of Lincoln.

Fiefs and Feudal Tenures

According to a charter quoted by de la Croix (vol. i., p. 134), who gives Jeune as his authority, the fief of Samarès was granted by William Rufus to Rodolph de St. Helier in 1095; but this charter seems to be of doubtful authenticity, and, even if genuine, cannot be of earlier date than the thirteenth century. At the Court of Common Pleas held in Jersey in 1300, Peter de Sausmarez, Seigneur of Samarès, son of Peter de St. Helier, was summoned to answer by what warrant he claims to have "in his Manor de Sausmarez" these rights : "That of jurisdiction—*i.e.*, to keep a Paire of Gallows; of having a Warren; of Wreck; of a Free Liberty to chase after Rabbits, and (to keep) Hawks, which are Regaltys belonging to the Dignity of the King."[1] Whereupon the said Peter replied : "That he and his Ancestors were in possession from time immemorial of the said Manor . . . and had Free Liberty to chase after Rabbits over all the Mount of St. Hellier, with their Hunting Dogs, Ferrets, Nets and Hunting Poles . . . and of the regalities aforesaid, as the appurtenances of the same, and offers to justify it.

In 1331 the fief belonged to Guillaume de St. Helier,[2] but for his treachery during the French invasion of the Islands it was confiscated by Edward III. in favour of Geoffrey de Thoresby, who sold it to Sir John Maltravers, Governor of the Islands, and he disposed of it

[1] Abridged from an old English translation among the MSS. of Lord de Saumarez, extracted from the Exchequer Records.

[2] Extent of 1331.

to Philip de Barentin, who, as we have already seen, sold it to Guillaume Payn at the time when he sold Rosel to Raoul Lemprière. De La Croix[1] gives a curious list from an old manuscript of the services required of the vassals of Samarès by their seigneurs. Besides the usual services of cartage, cleaning out the barns and colombier, and "suite de Cour," they were expected to "defend him with their bodies in the battlefield, and and be his surety, body for body if requisite;[2] and to convey him to the four ports of Normandy once in his life, or in theirs. Should the seigneur reside on the Fief du Hommet, a dependency of the Fief de Samarès, the priest was obliged to convey the lady of the manor to the church on a white horse the day she went to be churched."

The fief passed by marriage into the hands of the Dumaresqs, one of the oldest and most distinguished Jersey families. In 1501 the King's Procureur, Raulin le Marquand, insisted that John Dumaresq should erect a gallows on his fief for the execution of Pierre Resde, as it afforded a more extensive view, and thus would be more exemplary to the people than the market-place of St. Helier.[3]

Samarès remained in the possession of the Dumaresq family until the reign of William and Mary, when it was presented by Deborah Dumaresq, heiress of that branch of the family, to Mr. John Seale. It passed

---

[1] Vol. i., p. 135.
[2] "Et le plaiger corps pour corps si le cas le requiert."
[3] De la Croix, t. i., p. 123.

MARKET PLACE, GUERNSEY.

Fiefs and Feudal Tenures

subsequently to the Hammonds and Mourants, and has recently been sold to Mr. Davis.

The Manor of Trinity was held by the de St. Martins from the earliest times.[1] They descended from a Drouet de St. Martin, who, according to the Extent of 1274, was accused of having usurped certain lands in the parishes of St. Pierre-du-Bois and Torteval, in Guernsey, "since the time Dru de Barentin was Bailiff," and also of taking certain lands in the parish of Trinity, Jersey, which belonged to the King. Henry de St. Martin, son of Drouet, Bailiff of Jersey in 1318, was a Seigneur of Trinity, and so was the John de St. Martin who was murdered by the two de Barentins about the year 1370. In 1515 Thomas de St. Martin died childless, and the manor descended to his sister's son, Drouet Lemprière.

The seigneurie remained in the Lemprière family until Catherine, heiress of Gilles Lemprière, married Amias de Carteret, Bailiff of Guernsey from 1601 to 1631. To this branch of the de Carterets it belonged until the death of Sir Philip Carteret-Silvester, when it passed to his sister Caroline, on whose marriage to the Count Gabriel Henry de St. George, it passed into the de St. George family.

Towards the middle of the nineteenth century it was bought by Colonel Swan, whose son, in 1910, sold it to Mr. Athelstan Riley, by whom it has been practically rebuilt. The seigneur owes, as part of his tenure, the service of two Mallards, should the King visit the

[1] *Armorial*, p. 130.

The Channel Islands

island, and this service was duly performed by Mr. Riley in July, 1921. For, during the Royal visit, His Majesty was conducted to the States House, and there those Jersey seigneurs owing direct homage to the King appeared before him, and the Seigneur de St. Ouen—as principal seigneur—knelt, with his hands in the King's, and said the old Norman formula, which his ancestors had sworn to the Dukes themselves—the others repeating after him: "Sire, je suis votre homme lige [1] à vous porter foy et hommage contre tous." For this homage, to the seigneurs in both islands, His Majesty sent a formal receipt for "l'hommage qu'il m'en doit pour et à cause du franc fief de (name of fief inserted)" "en l'isle de" ("Jersey" or "Guernsey" inserted) "parcelle de nôtre duché de Normandie."

It is impossible here to dwell on the minor fiefs and their owners, or the curious tenures by which some were held, such as the Fief des Augrès, whose seigneur, on the occasion of the marriage of his eldest son, owed the heir of Dièlament a fat white lamb; or the Tapon estate, a dependency of the Fief de Bagot, belonging for centuries to the Millais family, which owed to its seigneur a pair of white gloves, three hens, three loaves, and a capon; and we must turn to the fiefs and seigneurs of the sister island of Guernsey.

A nearly straight line drawn across Guernsey from Pleinmont Point at the extreme south-west to Fort Doyle at the extreme north-east would almost exactly divide the island into its two original fiefs. We will

[1] The word "lige" was not used in Guernsey.

38

Fiefs and Feudal Tenures

first deal with the portion lying south-east of the line, which comprises the parishes of St. Sampson's, St. Peter-Port, St. Martin's, St. Andrew's, Forest, and part of Torteval. All this was the original fief of the Néels de St. Sauveur, Vicomtes of Le Cotentin, who probably built the Château des Marais to serve as a Manor House; but in 1048 they rebelled against their Duke, and he gave their lands to the Abbey of Marmoutier which retained the advowsons of the six parish churches even after the land had again been restored to its original owners, and also in later days when it was subdivided into a number of smaller fiefs.[1]

Of these the principal were Anneville, Sausmarez, and Blanchelande. There were besides certain manors owned by various noble Norman families, such as the de Barnevilles, le Bouteilliers, de St. Remys, de Beauchamps, and de Rosels, which, by reason of the adherence of their owners to the cause of Normandy, had escheated to the King before the Extent of 1331 was made, so that he is, to this day, one of the largest fief-holders in Guernsey.

The land was divided into large farms called *bordages*.[2] The parish of St. Peter-Port, for instance, contained six of these bordages, and the names they still bear generally refer to their original holders in the years 1299 and 1331.

The tenants were called *bordiers* and were hereditary

[1] Dupont, t. i., p. 241 ; and miscellaneous documents in Bibliothèque Nationale de Paris.

[2] From an old French word *borde*, meaning a house.

officers. They had to attend the Chief Pleas, and to form the guard of the prisoners at executions. Each bordier had to maintain a farmhouse; surrounding each house were the plough lands (caruées), which were divided into long strips called ox-gangs (bouvées), which, curiously enough, vary in size, those of the Fief le Roi at St. Martin being 100 vergées, while those at St. Peter-Port are 130. (Vergées are a local measurement of land, and are two-fifths of an acre in size.) A common plough tilled the whole field, drawn by oxen furnished by each bouvée. When the crop of wheat or flax was taken up, the church got the tithe, then the lord of the manor got his dues, or *campart*, and the rest belonged to the tenant, who had to pay a couple of fowls every year on the ground occupied by his house and garden, as a substitute for the campart. This due, called *poulage*, still exists. It was not until the seventeenth century that the tenants were allowed to enclose their lands, nor until 1857 that the office of the bordiers was finally abolished; the only three seigneurs whose fiefs were of sufficient importance to have bordiers being the King, the Seigneur of Le Comte, and the Abbot of St. Michel.

Many of the smaller Courts are still held in the open-air. Here and there in a roadside hedge or in a farm-yard can be seen a stone bench, that few would guess to be the site of a manorial court. One of the most picturesque of these is in a steep-paved lane leading down from the churchyard of St. Saviour; another in the northern part of the Castel churchyard.

Fiefs and Feudal Tenures

Like the other seigneurs, the King had the rights of *fouage*, or hearth tax; *pasnage*, a due paid to the seigneur for the right to pasture pigs in the woods belonging to the manor; *verp*, or a duty on all ownerless beasts straying into his pastures; a percentage or "triezième" on all transfers or successions of land on his fiefs; and in the case of his lands bordering on the seashore, he also had rights called *varech*, or wreck of the sea, claimed on all *débris* thrown up on the beach, and *esperquerie*, or the due paid to the Crown by the tenants for the pre-emption of congers.

Fishing was, in those days, the principal means of livelihood for the poorer classes, who salted and dried the fish and sold them to the people of England and Normandy for eating during the many days when the Church commanded abstention from meat. While being dried, the fish were split open and hung to dry on poles or pieces of stick *(des perches)*, hence the name *esperquerie*, which is found nowhere else but in the Islands.

In 1331 the King had no warren in the island, but he or his representative had the right of chase outside the limits of the warrens of Guillaume de Chesney and Matthew de Sausmarez, and also might exercise this right a day earlier than any other seigneur. He also claimed the right of a market where his own weights and measures were used. This market was held, not in the town, as at present, but at Les Landes in the Castel parish. Both the Abbot of the Vale and the Seigneur of Le Comte disputed this right, and claimed to have their own markets and their own weights, but according to a Close Roll of 1308 the matter was settled in favour of the King.[1]

Among his other possessions were the three Royal castles, Cornet, Vale, and Orgueil or des Marais, and nine mills, both wind and water. His tenants had to carry his corn to his grange, and when the corn was to be exported to France, they had to find the crew and the boat in which it was conveyed; they also had to keep the mills in repair, the King furnishing the necessary iron and wood.

The King also had the right of taking silken robes and scarlet mantles. He possessed in St. Peter-Port a "certain manor called the Grange," where his wheat and other dues were stored under the superintendence of his "Receiver." Attached to this was the Chapel "de la Grange," in which Masses for the souls of his ancestors were said daily. This manor and chapel were most probably situated in the vicinity of the Tour Gand, a fortress which defended the approaches of the town on the north, as the Tour Beauregard (situated where St. Barnabas's Church now stands) did on the south.

In the seventeenth century the "King's barn," attached to this manor, was converted into the Royal Court House, and used as such until 1799; it is known as "La Plaiderie" to this day. In connection with this manor was a colombier, but this was only valued at four sols in 1331, as all the doves had flown. The

---

[1] Publication Spéciale de Société Jersiaise, 1902, p. 14 ; and 9me Publication ditto, p. 78.

Fiefs and Feudal Tenures

islanders on their part were exempt from all further taxes, except to redeem the King should he be put in prison ("dou Diex le gart"), and from all military services out of the Islands, except the reconquest of England should it revolt against their Dukes.[1]

There were many disputes respecting the feudal liberties of the Islands in regard to their Sovereign, the gist of most of them being: "Who shall decide what dues are owed by the King's tenants—the King in his courts in London, or the tenants through their jurats in the Islands?" The King ultimately gave way, leaving the tenants masters of the situation, and by degrees their personal services diminished until not a trace of them now remains.

The Fief d'Anneville was, in 1248, granted by King Henry III. to William de Chesney. His manor-house of Anneville, situated on the western side of St. Sampson's parish, exists, though in a sadly changed condition, as a farmhouse, and there the Court of Anneville is held. The old triple-arched doorway, so like the west door of the Vale Church, survives, and at the back of the house are the ruins of the old manorial chapel dedicated to St. Thomas. The de Chesneys being also seigneurs of the superior fief of Le Comte, Anneville in several instances fell to junior members of the family, and in 1350 we find Sir Edmund de Chesney, Governor of the Island, while consenting to the fief belonging to his younger brother, especially reserving to himself the right of residence in the manor-

[1] Dupont, t. ii., 214, and Extent of 1248.

The Channel Islands

house of Anneville whenever he should be in Guernsey.
Sir Edmund's youngest sister, Joan, married Denis le
Marchant, Lieutenant-Bailiff of Guernsey, and another
sister, Eleanor, married first a de Garis, and secondly
that Geoffrey Wallis of Jersey whose manor-house and
lands were submerged in the great storm of 1395.

This fief remained in the hands of the de Chesneys until Sir Robert Willoughby, afterwards Lord
Willoughby de Broke (son of Anne de Chesney, daughter and co-heiress of Sir Edmund de Chesney of
Brooke), sold it on February 16, 1509-10, " to Nicholas
Fouaschin fils Thomas," a member of an old Guernsey
family hailing from the parish of St. Pierre-du-Bois.

The purchaser of Anneville was one of the Gentlemen
Ushers to King Henry VIII.; he migrated to Southampton in 1510, and there his name became anglicised to
Fachin or Fashion. The fief remained in his family for
one hundred and fifty years, until Alice Fashion
("Dame d'Anneville"), only child of Thomas Fashion,
married Charles Andros in 1660 and brought it into the
Andros family, in whose hands it still remains. Of this
ancient family, many of whom fought and died for their
king and country, Sir Edmund Andros, nephew of the
Charles Andros who married Alice Fashion, was the
most distinguished member. He was a major of
Dragoons, and was sent to America and made Governor-
General of the province of New York in 1674, in spite
of his having been made Bailiff of his native island in
that year. He was promoted to be Governor-in-Chief
of New England in 1686, and Governor of Virginia and

PETIT BOT BAY, GUERNSEY.

Fiefs and Feudal Tenures

all the American Colonies in 1692. After his return from America he was made Governor of Guernsey, 1704-6. He died in 1713, leaving no descendants, and his estates were inherited by his nephews and nieces.

Excepting the de Carterets of St. Ouen, the family of de Sausmarez of Sausmarez Manor may claim a longer connection with their fief than any other seigneur in the Islands.

At what date the "châtellenie" of Jerbourg was added to the seigneurie of Sausmarez is unknown, but in 1299 at the assizes held at St. Peter-Port Matthew de Sausmarez, then a minor, son and heir of Matthew de Sausmarez defunct, with his guardians, Thomas d'Estefeldt [1] and Robert Blondel, acknowledged that he held his fief of Sausmarez from the Crown, as his ancestors had done from time immemorial, by the service of being third cup-bearer to the King, relief, and presence at three Chief Pleas.

This Matthew claimed the castle of Jerbourg, which was confirmed to him by Edward III. in 1330, on condition that in time of war the "men of the commonalty of the said Island shall be received there with their goods and chattels." And in this castle Matthew might hold his court, with his sheriff and his vavasseurs, who "would execute his justice for him, and owed him certain spurs valued twelve sols tournois"; he also was entitled to "the wreck of the sea, free warren, right of chase, and

[1] His stepfather, married to Alice de St. Remy, heiress to her brother William de St. Remy, Bailiff of Guernsey, and widow of Matthew de Sausmarez senior.

his windmill, to which his men ought to bring timber and millstones at their own cost." His tenants were also " bound to carry the corn and oats of the said Matthew to Normandy wheresoever he shall wish, between St. Michael's Mount and Vauville," at his cost; and should Matthew or his heirs " wish to be carried over to the Island of Jersey the said tenants are bound to take him across at their own cost for three sols tournois and one dinner,"[1] which points to an early connection between the two seigneuries of Sausmarez in the two Islands. This duty of the tenants to carry their lord over to Jersey was insisted upon in 1798 by the then seigneur of the fief. But he found that the tenant of that period was less docile than the serf of the fourteenth century, and the attempt has not been repeated.

Only a few trenches and grass-grown dykes now mark the spot where once stood the castle of Jerbourg guarding the isthmus of that name, but His Majesty was taken to the site during the Royal visit of 1921, and Sir Havilland de Sausmarez, Seigneur of Sausmarez, now Bailiff of Guernsey, as " third cup-bearer to the King whensoever he should visit the Island," provided the cups and handed His Majesty his tea (for by Royal command so his service was commuted) during the afternoon, while his wife, Dame Annie de Sausmarez, G.B.E., performed the same service to the Queen.

The fief continued in the family of de Sausmarez until the reign of Henry VIII., when John Andros (or Andrews), a young Englishman who came to the island in

[1] Publication Spéciale de la Société Jersiaise for 1902, pp. 91-4, etc.

Fiefs and Feudal Tenures

the suite of Sir Peter Meautis, Governor of Guernsey, married, in 1543, Judith de Sausmarez, eventual heiress of the seigneurie. Through this marriage it remained in the Andros family two hundred years, and, as we have seen, they also owned the Fief d'Anneville.

Thomas Andros, a grandson of this John Andros and Judith de Sausmarez, married Elizabeth de Carteret, daughter of Amias de Carteret, Seigneur of Trinity, Bailiff of Guernsey, and of Catherine Lemprière, his wife.

The eldest son of Amias Andros, Sir Edmund, who has been already mentioned, had two brothers, John and George, and it was John's grandson, Charles Andros, who in 1748 sold the seigneurie of Sausmarez and the "Châtellenie" de Jerbourg to John de Sausmarez, and thus allowed the manor to revert to the descendants in the male line of its original owners. This Charles Andros had married Marie Fiott, sister of the rector of St. Martin's parish, eight years previously, and his wife having no child, he had small compunction in parting with his inheritance; but less than a year after the sale his eldest son was born. Therefore, in the bitterness of her spirit, his wife—like the Archbishop in the *Morte d'Arthur*—cursed "in the best manner and the most rguilous" the mill of Sausmarez—in those days the emblem of seigneurial prosperity—"that never again should it grind the tenants' oats or the seigneur's wheat." Her curse is said to have been fulfilled, and now the old mill stands idle and forlorn, bereft of its sails, a silent witness of the vengeance of a woman.

The Channel Islands

The John de Sausmarez who thus bought back the manor, and from whom its present owners are descended, was uncle of the famous Admiral Sir James Saumarez,[1] who, for his eminent services, was created a baronet and nominated a K.B. in 1801, and thirty years later, on the occasion of the coronation of William IV., was raised to the peerage as Baron de Saumarez. Of him Captain Mahan, the well-known authority on naval history, says: "For cool, steady courage, for high, professional skill, for patient, sustained endurance, Saumarez was unsurpassed."[2]

The Norman abbey of Blanchelande was founded in 1154 by Richard de la Haye and Matilda, daughter of William de Vernon, his wife. The arms of de la Haye —argent, a sun in its splendour—were adopted by the Abbey in memory of its founder.[3] Its possessions in Guernsey dated from 1199, when John, then Earl of Mortain and Seigneur of the Islands, gave it a prebend of Cherbourg, which included ninety acres[4] of land in Guernsey in the neighbourhood of Saints Bay, in St. Martin's parish. There the Abbot established the Priory of Martinvast, whose head, Robert Toulissac, in 1332, proved his claim to the usual seigneurial rights and to a mill, which, in 1217, had been granted to the Abbey by Robert le Bouteillier, son of Ralph. In 1267 the

[1] The name was thus anglicised by the Admiral when he entered the English Navy during the war with France.

[2] *Atlantic Monthly* for 1893, p. 618.

[3] *Archives de la Manche*, Série H. Abbaye de Blanchelande, p. 19.

[4] "Une caruée et demie": the present computation is 584 vergées or 281 acres.

MOYE POINT, NEAR LE GOUFFRE, GUERNSEY

Fiefs and Feudal Tenures

Abbot of Marmoutier abandoned to the Abbot of Blanchelande his patronage or right of advowson of St. Martin's Church, and this right was, in 1323, successfully maintained by the then Abbot, supported by John le Marchant, Bailiff, and the Royal Court, against King Edward II.

The Priory was situated at the top of the road leading to Saints' Bay, on the right-hand side; the farmhouse now standing there is said to have been built from its stones. This house was given its present name by Edward Mauger, who was taken prisoner by Algerian corsairs in the reign of William III., and sold into slavery in Barbary. Having been ransomed by his sister, on his return he called his house "La Barbarie" in memory of his sufferings. A large cross or "Calvary" stood in a neighbouring field, which still bears the name "Croisie."

Like all other alien priories, this property was confiscated by Henry V.; and in 1563 it was sold by the Royal Commissioners to Nicholas Carey for £20 sterling and a little over ten quarters of annual wheat rent.[1] All the other ecclesiastical properties in the island—such as those belonging to the Abbots of St. Michel and Marmoutier and the Abbess of Caen— have been retained by the Crown; and it is a curious fact that at the Chief Pleas, when the list of Crown fiefs is read out, the names of the original owners are preserved. For instance, "L'Abbé de Mont St. Michel" or "L'Abbesse de Caen" is called out, and in

[1] Dupont, t. ii., pp. 109-10.

The Channel Islands

Guernsey the Procureur (in Jersey the Lieutenant-Governor) makes answer, "Sa Majesté."

Nicholas Carey, the purchaser of Blanchelande, belonged to a family long established in the Islands. When the Careys came to Guernsey is not known, but in the Assize Rolls of 1288 a John Karee is described as "Coustumier [1] en la Cour du Roi et en la Cour de l'Eglise," [2] and was accused in 1323 of "causing certain parishioners to be summoned before the Ecclesiastical Court on pleas which belong of right to the King's Court," for which he was convicted and "put at the King's mercy." Philip Carée held lands in St. Martin's parish in 1309 and 1331, and a John Carée in 1364 and 1399; which lands are known to have been held fifty years later by the direct ancestors of the Carey family. [3] The name of Carrey is also found in the early records of Normandy and Brittany, and was borne by two of the defenders of Mont St. Michel.

Nicholas himself was Seigneur du Mourier in Jersey in right of Catherine Perrin, his grandmother, Co-Seigneur of Ste. Hélène and Seigneur of Mauxmarquis, as well as being a jurat, Queen's Receiver, and Procureur or Attorney-General.

[1] An office said to be analogous to that of the present King's Receiver.

[2] Rot. Miscel. $1\frac{30}{71}$ Exchequer (Treasury). This roll is endorsed "La Bellouse, a parish in one of the Channel Islands"; St. Martin's parish in Guernsey being always known in ancient deeds as "St. Martin de la Bellouse," *Beilleuse* to this day being the name of the district surrounding St. Martin's Church.

[3] Colonel J. H. C. Carey's MSS.

Fiefs and Feudal Tenures

The Court of Blanchelande is held in the house standing upon the site of the old Priory ; its owner, instead of paying " chef rente," being obliged by his tenure to supply a room in which the Court can assemble. The Court consists of a sénéchal, a greffier, a prévost, and three vavasseurs : of these there were originally six, called the vavasseurs " Hervy, Durant, Capis, Au Claire, Becville, and Au Seigneur," but these old names are now obsolete.[1]

The tenant of Fief Durant, one of the dependencies of Blanchlande, owes the seigneur a donkey and a cake made of a bushel of wheat.[2]

In 1331 Bruneaux de St. Martin owed military service of one knight; Rohais, like Anneville, had to keep a prison for the service of the Court. Burhons and Aufay owed, one a pair of gilt spurs of five sous tournois, the other a pair of white spurs or twelve deniers tournois; the land is called Les Eperons to this day, and its present owner, Miss Rougier, paid her feudal dues in person to His Majesty during his visit to the island in 1921.

We now come to the portion of the island lying north-west of a line drawn from Fort Doyle to Plein-

[1] From Mr. John Allez's MSS., as vavasseur of Blanchelande.

[2] In 1887 the prévôt of Blanchelande brought an action against three of the tenants for payment of " one fowl, one half and one sixteenth of a fowl, one fortieth and one four hundred and eightieth part of a fowl, twenty-eight eggs, and three-fourths and one-eighth of an egg," fivepence being the usual fine for non-payment. Judgment was given for the plaintiffs by default (Guernsey *Star*, April 26, 1887).

mont. As we have already seen, early in the eleventh century Guernsey was divided into two great fiefs belonging respectively to Néel, Vicomte de St. Sauveur, and to Anchetil, Vicomte de Bessin. The four parishes with which we are about to deal were the property of Anchetil. They subsequently escheated to the Dukes of Normandy, and were subdivided, in nearly equal portions, between the Abbey of Mont St. Michel and the descendants of Anchetil, who were subsequently created Earls of Chester; the lands held by the Abbey being called Fief St. Michel, and those held by the Earl, Fief le Comte. In the days of Geoffrey of Anjou these lands were granted to Geoffrey Wake, whose descendant Hugh Wake, on February 3, 1239-40, disposed of his ancestral estates in Guernsey to Baldwin de Vere. Twenty-three years later the de Veres sold the fief to Sir William de Chesney and Felicia his wife.

Sir William, as we have seen, had already been given the fief of Anneville. His seal, dated 1253, *Sigillum Wil(lel)mi Chainé*, bearing "four fusils in fesse," and thus having a curious affinity to the arms of the d'Albinis and de Carterets,[1] is in the Bibliothèque Nationale.

Sir Nicholas de Chesney, his eldest son, was Governor of the Islands in 1294 and 1297, and so was his grandson, Sir Edmund de Chesney.

Of his granddaughters, married, one to a de Garis

[1] The arms seem subsequently to have been differenced by each fusil being charged with escallop sable.

and the other to Denis le Marchant, mention has already been made. The Fief le Comte, together with the Fief d'Anneville, was sold in 1509 by Sir Robert Willoughby, heir, through his mother, of the de Chesneys, to Nicholas Fouaschin, and for another hundred and fifty years the two fiefs remained united under the same seigneur. The Fief le Comte was undoubtedly the most important in the island. Its seigneurs owned " chapels, colombiers, warrens, fish-ponds, varech, mills, the chase of hares and rabbits, and free market on Les Landes ";[1] and three sous were payable to the lord of the manor on the marriage of any tenant's daughter.

The Court of Le Comte, consisting of a sénéchal, eight vavasseurs, a greffier, and three sergeants (or bordiers), still meet in a small building near St. George. Before the old chapel of St. George was destroyed, the Court was held there. Until comparatively recent times it was the recording Court for all contracts relating to property on the fief, and retained its rights as a Petty Court for debts and minor police cases. It has a seal of its own, which is still in existence. In 1597 Thomas Fashion claimed that this seal had been given by John Earl of Mortain, and that it represented Sampson d'Anneville; but according to Sir Edgar MacCulloch it " dates from about the beginning of the fifteenth century, and represents a knight on foot in full plate armour in the act of drawing or sheathing his sword; the nimbus round his head and the letters

---

[1] Evidence given by Thomas Fashion before Queen Elizabeth's Commissioners in 1597 (Fief le Comte MSS.).

The Channel Islands

'S.G.' above his shoulders leave no doubt that the figure is intended to represent St. George." [1]

In 1629 Fief St. George, then a dependency of Fief le Comte, was sold by George Fashion to Nicholas de Jersey, whose only child Marie married Jacques Guille in 1638, and so brought this fief into the Guille family, whose descendant, the Rev. H. G. de C. Steven Guille, sold it, in 1921, to Mr. J. H. Sebire.

The Fief le Comte was, in 1630, sold by George Fashion to Peter Priaulx, one of the few Guernseymen who, during the Wars of the Commonwealth, were partisans of the Stuarts. In 1644 Priaulx was accused of being involved in a plot for " seizing the places called Gerbourg and the Castle of the Valle; and by this means to keep strong there for Sir P. Osborne "; [2] the said Peter Osborne being a staunch Royalist and then engaged in holding Castle Cornet for the King and shelling the island, which was Republican. By the irony of fate, a shell from the castle (at that time commanded by Sir Baldwin Wake) struck and killed Peter Priaulx in 1650. His great-grandson, Thomas Priaulx, sold the fief in 1722 to Eleazar le Marchant, and through the le Marchants it passed to the great-grandmother of the present seigneur, Colonel Thomas Hutchesson.

There has been abolished only within the last forty-five years a curious *redevance* due to the seigneur of this fief by his tenants whose lands bordered on Vazon

[1] Notices of old Guernsey churches and chapels in St. Peter-Port parish magazine for 1874-5.
[2] Actes des États, p. 258.

Bay—namely, a yearly payment of one double [1] per pig on each pig reared. For this payment the tenants were originally entitled to send their pigs to graze in the now submerged Forest of Vazon, of which possibly vestiges remained in and about Vazon Bay after the creation of Fief le Comte.[2]

The Priory of St. Michel-du-Valle was a dependency of the famous Abbey of Mont St. Michel in Normandy.

To the south-east of the Vale Church is an old farm-house still bearing the name of L'Abbaye, and doubtless standing on the site of the original Priory, which was in a ruinous state as early as the reign of Henry IV., for we find Sir John de Lisle, Governor of Guernsey, in 1406 asking permission to use the timber of the buildings for the repairs of Castle Cornet, "as the Priory had fallen into decay."

The Priory had the largest feudal Court of all the seigneuries, consisting of a sénéchal, eleven vavasseurs, a greffier, six bordiers, and a wand-bearer, or *porte-lance*. The official seal of the fief represented the Archangel Michael trampling Satan under foot.

One of the principal duties of this Court was to see that the King's highway was kept in proper order, and for this purpose the officers of the Court, mounted on horseback, accompanied by thirty-six *pions*, or footmen, and various Crown officers, had to ride round the accustomed highways once in three years, and every obstacle encountered by the wand of the porte-lance—eleven

---

[1] A local copper coin, value one-eighth of a penny.
[2] From Mr. John le Mottée's MS.

and a quarter feet long—had to be cleared away. These processions, called *chevauchées*, were attended by many curious rites and customary observances, one of them being the immemorial privilege of the pions—who were chosen for their good looks—of kissing every woman they met, whatever her degree, though only one pion was allowed to kiss the same lady. The Abbot owed three dinners a year to the Crown officers,[1] and had to provide them with three horses and two "valets" for the chevauchée, for which also he had to provide the dinner; but he could insist that a Saturday (the market-day) should intervene between the dates of deciding on and celebrating this event, so that he might be able to provide the necessary provisions.[2]

The last chevauchée took place in Guernsey on May 31, 1837, and the Court itself was abolished soon after. The Jersey equivalent of this chevauchée is called "La Visite Royale des Chemins et Sentes publics."

Many curious old feudal *redevances*, or rent services, are to be found in old deeds and "Livres de Perchage." A chaplet of roses on St. John's Day (June 24) is pretty often met with. Among the possessions of Denis le Marchant in 1393 was a rent of this character payable by John Benest.[3] In 1615 we find a later Denis le Marchant suing Jean Olliver, junior, "à cause de sa femme" for a "chapeau de roses." And in 1618 Thomas Lemprière, of Jeresey, bought a rent of a

---

[1] This right was renounced by Henry III. in 1218.
[2] Dupont, t. ii., p. 234.
[3] " Bille de Partage " of Denis le Marchant, 1393.

Fiefs and Feudal Tenures

" bracelet or chaplet of roses, containing as many roses as are necessary to make a wreath, the said wreath to be the thickness of a man's arm or head," [1] while the Channel Islands themselves were granted by Henry VI. to Henry de Beauchamp, Duke of Warwick, " for the yearly rent of a red rose to be payd on Midsummer Day."

A still more curious rent was that owed by Thomas Sandre, who was brought before the Royal Court of Guernsey in June, 1591, and ordered to pay "devant soleil couché," on pain of imprisonment, to " Mr. Jean de Sausmarez fils Colin," a dozen butterflies.

Nor have all these quaint payments yet become obsolete. To this day Sieur A. Breton, of St. Saviour, pays the heirs of the late Miss E. Guille, of St. George, 4s. 3½d. a year, "èquivalent" of "une chartée de cendres" (a cartload of ashes); and a Mrs. Bourgaize pays 4s. 6d. a year, representing eighteen eels, to the heirs of Mr. Allez.

[1] The Rev. J. A. Messervy's MSS.

CHAPTER IV

LAW COURTS AND OFFICIAL SEALS

STARTING no doubt from similar constitutions, the two principal islands have, in the course of time, diverged considerably from one another. Each, indeed, has its Lieutenant-Governor, Bailiff, Dean, States Assembly, and Royal Court, but the rights and privileges of the principal officers and assemblies vary exceedingly.

As is proved by Stapleton's "Norman Rolls," up to the year 1177, and for how long previously we know not, Jersey and Guernsey formed one unit, administered by Robert d'Agneaux as deputy for William de Courcy, Seneschal of Normandy. It was only after William de Courcy's death that their separate government began. In 1179 we find that, although Jersey was divided into three districts *(ministeria)*, each with a separate administrator, Guernsey already had her *Curia regis*, or Royal Court, with its own official seal, and presided over by a Vicomte, then named Gilbert de la Hougue, who had also been administrator of a Jersey district. Alderney and Sark were then under separate jurisdictions.

In Guernsey, for many centuries, the office of Vicomte has been suppressed; his criminal jurisdiction having been merged into that of the Prevôt or Sheriff, while his political powers have lapsed into those of the Bailiff. Jersey retains the two officials, although, owing to the conflict of jurisdictions, Vicomtes were abolished in France in 1749. But in Jersey the Bailiff's office has long been the more important of the two, as gradually the representative of Ducal and Civil Law has ousted the old feudal appeal to "combat judiciaire" which Norman common sense eventually realised did not always favour right as against might.

But the Constitutions of the Islands are generally attributed to King John, who, after the loss of Normandy, naturally tried to retain the loyalty of what had become an important outpost of his kingdom. We learn from the Assize Roll of 1309 that he twice visited the Islands in person, both to repel invasions of the French and to divert their administration from Normandy to home rule, by granting them the right of electing their own jurats and other important privileges of self-government. He also instituted an organised force for local defence similar to the communal militia of the Norman free towns. Even then the Islands possessed local franchises and liberties with regard to trade, weights and measures, and feudal usages, and also the important privileges of exemption from all military services out of the Islands except under the personal command of the Duke of Normandy if it was found necessary to reconquer England, and exemption from all contributions to the Crown in return for a specified yearly payment of £70 tournois. Their amended Constitutions were based on the old "Droit-Normand," itself an inheritance of Scandinavian legislation with a substratum of Roman law on which had been grafted certain feudal observances, and, more especially, the principle of "Nulle terre sans seigneur."

As time went on King John's successors tried to impose English laws upon the Islanders by sending over itinerant judges, who claimed to administer justice without the assistance of the respective Bailiffs and jurats. Moreover, Edward I. insisted on his newly invented Pleas of "Quo Warranto" being introduced, while government officials—appointed from England—endeavoured to tamper with local usage and custom. But naturally then—as ever—these attempts were fiercely resented by the inhabitants, who declared that they were governed "ni par la Loi de Normandie, ni par celle d'Angleterre," but, as from time immemorial, by their own laws and customs. After a constitutional struggle which lasted for half a century, the following franchises, claimed as a right in 1333, and which still form the basis of the Islands' constitutions, were confirmed by Royal Charter in 1341 and ratified by successive sovereigns.

The principal among them are these:

That each island should elect their jurats from among the islanders themselves; that these jurats should have power to judge all civil and criminal cases, excepting high treason and—in Guernsey—coining, crimes which were reserved for the King in Council to deal with. That no islander may be cited or tried out of his island; that islanders are exempt from all taxes, tolls, levies, and contributions exacted by England; and that homage is only due when the King visits the Islands in person.[1]

In Jersey (where they wear scarlet mantles) the jurats are elected by those ratepayers who are British subjects. No special legal training is required in their case, nor even in that of the Bailiff—indeed, in 1832 the Court asserted that it was not necessary to study for the law in order to become a good judge in Jersey, but that the knowledge of the principal laws was best achieved by long practice in business. Certain callings, however, such as those of butcher, baker, brewer, or publican, are disqualifications, and, according to ancient custom, nobody ought to be elected a jurat who does not own at least forty quarters of wheat rent. In Guernsey (where the jurats wear purple robes), up to about 1582, they were elected by "the constables of each parish taking the voices of all the rate payers of their parish at the church door immediately after divine service;"[2] but now they are chosen by the Elective States. The jurats were formerly chosen only from the best born and richest men—as the Precepts d'Assize directs—"from the most notable and discreet, wise, loyal, and rich men of the island."

In the olden days there were certain privileges attached to the office. By a Guernsey Ordonnance of 1548 only jurats and rectors and a few other notable people might shoot hares and rabbits in the island, and

[1] See *Les Cours Royales des Iles Normandes*, by Julien Havet, pp. 231-3.

[2] Warburton's *Treatise on the History, etc., of Guernsey*, p. 52.

the jurats, with the Governor and Bailiff, were the first persons to be served with meat by the butchers. A jurat was also entitled to be addressed as " Monsieur " or " Écuyer " in Guernsey, and as "honnête homme " in Jersey, where, indeed, the slightly invidious decree was issued in 1610 that no man was to be called " honnête homme," except " gentilshommes ou officiers de la Cour Royale."[1]

Inasmuch, however, as the office of jurat lasts for a man's life, people have sometimes been elected who were unwilling to sit. Thus, in Guernsey, Jean de Vyvier was fined for this reason in 1304; and in 1798 Mr. John Tupper, having threatened to leave the island sooner than be sworn in after his election, was warned that should he do so he would be fined £100.

In Guernsey both the Bailiff and the jurats, by their oath of office, are bound to resist the Papal Supremacy, whereas in Jersey there are no religious disabilities.

The Royal Courts are the criminal tribunals in both islands, and have jurisdiction over all offences committed in their bailiwicks, except treason, coining, and laying violent hands on the Bailiffs or jurats, for which the punishments are reserved to the Crown. In Jersey, before the passing of the " Law on Criminal Procedure " in 1864, the criminal was, in serious cases, tried by a jury or "enditement" of thirteen police officers. If convicted, the prisoner could then demand the benefit of the Grande Enquête du Pays, numbering twenty-four. Since 1864 the jury always numbers twenty-four,

---

[1] Soc. Jers., 11me Bulletin, p. 127.

of which nine votes may acquit. There has never been a jury in civil cases. But though an "enquête du pays" was the custom in Guernsey up to the sixteenth century, the twelve jurats now constitute both judge and jury. French is, nominally, still the official language, but in both islands the use of English has recently been made optional in the local Parliament or "States."

The Jersey Court House, or Cohue Royale, is situated in the Market Place or Royal Square. It was originally a small thatched building erected in mediæval times; in 1542 the Vicomte was ordered to see that a bar was erected in front of the jurats' bench to prevent outsiders coming in to listen and interrupt by thrusting their heads between the jurats' knees. It was rebuilt by Sir George Carteret in 1647, and has lately been much enlarged and redecorated.

In Guernsey, up to the seventeenth century, justice was administered in various places—the Town Church, Castle Cornet, even in private houses, at the discretion of the Governor; eventually the King's barn in the Pollet was selected, which served the double purpose of a corn market and a Court House, and by a special Ordonnance was to be cleared at noon so that the market might commence. This locality was called from this circumstance La Plaiderie; in course of time this being found too small and inconvenient, the present building was erected in 1799 and enlarged in 1903.

The States in Jersey comprise the Lieutenant-Governor, the Bailiff, the twelve jurats, the twelve

HIGH STREET, ST. PETER-PORT, GUERNSEY.

rectors, the twelve constables, and seventeen deputies; and also the Crown officers, who are allowed to speak but not to vote. They date from the French occupation of the island under Pierre de Brezé, Comte de Mauleprier, 1461-68.

In Guernsey there are two "States," the Elective and the Deliberative. The former comprises the Royal Court and the parochial officers (such as constables, *douzeniers*, etc.), and numbers 243 members; the latter, being the legislative Assembly, consists of fifty-eight members only—the Bailiff, the twelve jurats, the ten rectors, the Procureur, the Comptroller, fifteen delegates and eighteen deputies; the Lieutenant-Governor may speak but cannot vote. In these States the island laws and taxes are passed, judicial and legislative powers being thus united. The earliest mention of a body resembling the States in Guernsey is a judgment of the Royal Court of March 1433-4, where we read that it was "ordonney et establie" by the Bailiff and jurats, with the counsel of "les gentilshommes" and of the "bonne Communauté de l'isle"; while a later deed, of March 26, 1480-1, referring to an assembly of representatives of the people of Guernsey to appoint attorneys to represent them in a dispute with the Admiral of France, shows this assembly to consist of the Lieutenant-Bailiff, jurats, clergy (or "gents d'église"), the constables of all the parishes, and "les plus sains des manants et habitans de l'isle." It will be observed that since 1434 "les gentilshommes" had disappeared and been replaced by the constables, and the clergy had been added. The States were again reconstituted in the seventeenth century.[1]

It is probable that these States were originally constituted on the model of the Trois États in Normandy, possibly during the interval between September 1338 and October 1340, when the French under Robert Bertram, Sire de Briquebec, occupied the island, the Bailiff and jurats corresponding with the noblesse, the rectors of the parish answering to the clergy, and the *douzaines*—an elected body in each parish—answering to the *tiers état*, or bourgeoisie.

Each of the two islands has its own laws, founded in Jersey in the first place on *Le Grand Coustumier de Normandie*—a work compiled in the thirteenth century—and, according to Sir Edward Coke, "compounded of some English laws given by Edward the Confessor and of divers customs of the Duchy of Normandy"—and in Guernsey on a treatise by Terrien, Lieutenant-Bailiff of Dieppe in the sixteenth century, which brought the Norman law down to the time of Queen Elizabeth. Besides these main sources of law, there are also in force various Royal Charters, Orders of the Sovereign in Council, Ordinances of the local Legislature, and such Statutes of the Realm as have been registered at the Greffes. In Guernsey the Ordinances framed by the Royal Court at once become law, but since 1771 the Jersey Court has been deprived of a similar privilege. The independence of the States of the two islands

[1] "Some Old Documents," article by Colonel de Guèrin in *Transactions of the Société Guernesiaise* for 1914.

Law Courts and Official Seals

was thus recognised by the great jurist, Sir Edward Coke: "The King's writ runneth not into these Isles . . . because the Courts there and those here go not by the same rule, method, or order of law, because these islands, though they are parcel of the Dominions of the Crown of England, yet they are not parcel of the Realm of England, nor, indeed, ever were: but were anciently parcel of the Duchy of Normandy, and are those Remains thereof, which all the powers of the Crown and Kingdom of France have not been able to wrest from England."

One of the most curious legal survivals in the Islands is the "Clameur de Haro." The legend—picturesque as it is—that the "Ha Ro" was an invocation to Rollo, first Duke of Normandy, to maintain justice among his people, has long been exploded. It is now generally agreed that this was originally but an outcome of the primitive cry of joy or terror, which developed elsewhere into "Hurrah!" of victory, or the "hue and cry" of distress.

As M. Pissard points out,[1] "Le haro n'était d'abord qu'une exclamation poussée par la victime et par les témoins d'un flagrant délit." This cry was developed by the Normans into a procedure destined to arrest immediately all criminal proceedings, and was a privilege specially reserved for the province of Normandy alone, so much so that, although an alien could exercise this custom in Normandy itself, yet a Norman could not avail himself of it outside the Duchy.[2]

[1] *La Clamour de Haro dans le Droit Normand*, Caen, 1911.
[2] *Op. cit.*, p. 117.

The Channel Islands

Although abolished in Normandy in 1583, yet, as proof of their Norman inheritance, it remains law in the Channel Islands to this day, though with slight local differences. In Jersey the appellant need only go on his knees, and before two witnesses, while kneeling on the ground, cry aloud, "Haro! Haro! Haro! A l'aide mon Prince, on me fait tort!" In Guernsey a religious tone has been introduced by the appellant and the witnesses—generally the two constables of the parish—reciting the Lord's Prayer in French at the conclusion of the above ceremony, which must then be put into writing and lodged at the Greffe within twenty-four hours. This is considered tantamount to an injunction to stay proceedings until the case is tried before the Court. It is a remarkable feature in this case that the prosecution is carried on by the Crown, and that the losing party, whether plaintiff or defendant, is mulcted in a small fine to the King, because the sacred cry of "Haro" is not to be carelessly invoked with impunity.

The succession to land and personal property differs in the two islands; and in Jersey only $2\frac{1}{4}$ vergées go to an acre, while in Guernsey there are $2\frac{1}{2}$.

In olden days many miserable wretches were banished, tortured, and burnt for reputed sorcery and witchcraft. The details of their examinations and confessions resemble all other recorded witch trials, which bears out the theory that such survivals of clandestine rites and customs are a record of the submerged and primitive creeds which the influx of more modern religions has

VIEW FROM OLD GOVERNMENT HOUSE HOTEL, GUERNSEY.

never wholly evicted from their strongholds in the minds of humanity.

It was not even considered necessary that accusations of witchcraft should be proved. Thus Jeanne Béhot, living in Alderney, was, in 1619, brought before Amias de Carteret, Bailiff of Guernsey and the Royal Court, on suspicion of witchcraft; and though after long imprisonment and repeated examinations nothing could be proved against her, yet "pour éviter au grand scandale et tremeur de ceux parmi lesquels elle a vescu cy-devant" she was condemned to perpetual banishment and her goods were sequestrated.[1]

In 1611 Pierre Guillart, for having purloined five pairs of woollen stockings from a boat bound for St. Malo, was condemned to twenty-four lashes, twelve at the carrefours of the town and twelve on the pier.[2]

Some of the instruments used for punishment were the pillory, the cage, and the stocks. In Guernsey the pillory and the cage used to stand in the small open space near the top of Cow Lane and opposite the north door of the Town Church, but about the year 1783 they

---

[1] Details of these trials are given in Sir Edgar MacCulloch's *Guernsey Folklore*, pp. 289-331, and in *Witchcraft and Devil-lore in the Channel Islands*, by Mr. J. Linwood Pitts.

[2] Much value was attached to woollen goods at that time. Up to the middle of the eighteenth century knitting was one of the principal industries of the Islands, and wool was the chief import. Everyone knitted—men, women, and children. A Jersey Act of Court of 1615 forbade Philip Picot to knit in company with young girls for fear of scandal, and ordered him, should he continue to knit, to do so in his own house and by himself.

were transferred to the neighbourhood of the present French Halles and Market Square. A new wooden cage, a narrow box of open woodwork, made to revolve on a stand, had to be built in 1650, the old one having been broken down by the cannon of Castle Cornet.[1]

In 1619 Jean le Normant, for having refused to submit to the sentence of the Guernsey Court—viz., that he should be exposed in the pillory to public view—had that sentence confirmed, and for his contumacy was further to receive twelve strokes of the whip from the Court House to the cage, and then to be put into the cage. In 1608 a man convicted of larceny was condemned to be flogged at every carrefour in St. Peter-Port till the blood came, to be attached to the pillory by one of his ears, of which the tip was to be subsequently cut off, and then to be banished. In 1614 Pierre Salmon, for stealing pea-sticks, was ordered to be at once put into the stocks until sunset, and on the next morning (Sunday), under pain of the whip, to go to his parish church of St. Pierre-du-Bois, and there to be put in the stocks from the beginning of matins until the end of the evening service—and they had long sermons in those days.

But the most curious sentence of all was that on Samuel Sauvary for stealing wheat in 1615. He was ordered to be flogged in the Vale School by the scholars, under the supervision of the Comptroller.[2]

In Guernsey, even as late as the beginning of last

[1] Elie Brevint's MSS. [2] Le Marchant MSS.

century, offenders convicted of petty larceny were marched scantily clad from the prison, accompanied by the bordiers, down High Street to the Market Place, and there attached to one of the pillars of the French Halles and publicly lashed by the executioner till the blood came.

An eyewitness thus describes a similar punishment which he saw inflicted in Jersey in 1829: "A naked, shrieking wretch with a cord round his neck, halberds pointed at his breast to prevent hurrying forward, his back streaming with blood, his face turned imploringly towards the surgeon, who walked behind the executioner, followed by a brutal and unsympathetic mob."[1]

The pillory and the stocks survived until about that date, and the cage even a little later; but now they have long since disappeared.

In the sixteenth century, when the influence of Calvinism began to be felt, all frivolities were severely repressed in both the islands. This policy was intended to supply a defect consequent upon the abolition of the old Church Courts, and proceeded upon the idea, handed down for ages, that penal laws were fitted to extinguish individual vice as well as to suppress social crime. After 1566 Ordinance after Ordinance was issued forbidding dancing and singing of worldly songs; and, finally, in 1583, it was decreed by the Royal Court of Guernsey that anyone found dancing or singing in public should be taken on the following Sunday to the nave of his parish church, and there, with his head, legs, and feet

[1] *Blackwood's Magazine*, vol. lxxxii., p. 223.

bare, clad only in a linen sheet, and holding a lighted torch in one hand, publicly do penance for his offence.

Sumptuary laws were also enacted—like those of the Scottish Parliament—to save the purses of "mony folk that are very unabill to sustain that coaste." In Guernsey, in 1574, maidservants or lodging-house keepers' daughters were forbidden to wear silver ornaments, muslin kerchiefs, velvets, or silks, excepting for the purpose of tying their garments together; and in Jersey they were not allowed to wear any lace worth more than sevenpence-halfpenny a yard. In 1631 the Puritans doubled the fine attached to this offence, and added that those who could not pay the fine were to be " sévèrement châtiées par le corps." [1]

For a long time the Islands had no official seal, but on November 15, 1279, Edward I. sent them one. This Royal seal disappeared long ago, but an impression of it is preserved in the National Archives of Paris. It bore the " three leopards passant " of England and the legend " S. Ballivie Insularum pro Rege Anglie." It was only used up to 1302, the time when Jersey and Guernsey each began to have its own Bailiff. Then the want of separate seals was felt, and before 1306 a seal was made for each separate bailiwick on the model of King Edward's seal, bearing the legend " S. Ballivie insule de Jeresie " and " de Gernereye " respectively. The latter bears above the shield a sprig, hitherto considered to be of laurel, or possibly of broom or " genista " representing the badge of the Plantagenets, although a recent ex-

[1] *Recueil d'Ordonnances*, pp. 52-3, etc.

amination of the fourteenth-century Guernsey seal reveals that what has hitherto been considered a "badge" is, in reality, merely the device—in this case a rose—which was always placed to separate the end from the beginning of an inscription, and has no heraldic significance whatever. For these arms were undoubtedly intended to be used as an official seal only, and it is most improbable that the King ever meant his own Royal Arms to be used as the personal arms of the Bailiwicks of Jersey and Guernsey; but, as this seal was never recalled and replaced by a new one, as were the Royal seals of England, it was evidently forgotten, and, in course of time, its heraldic meaning was forgotten also, so that the anomalous position exists that in both islands may be seen the Royal arms of England heading semi-official and even parochial announcements, such as elections of parish officers or requests for tenders for parish drains. Yet their legal right to do so would be difficult to dispute, for in the eighteenth century Privy Council authorised the Royal Mint to issue tokens bearing these arms for use in the Channel Islands, and, later on, when Privy Council authorised the minting of copper coins for Jersey and Guernsey respectively, this Royal shield, with the names of the respective islands underneath it, was officially ordained.

It has always been the custom in both islands for the Bailiffs to counterseal with their own arms the official seal of the bailiwick when affixed to contracts, just as in Guernsey the seneschals, especially those of St. Michel and Le Comte, used to counterseal the official seals of their fiefs; and it is these old impressions which are the earliest evidences the Islanders have of the antiquity of their arms.

The Islands were separated from Normandy too early to have their arms registered in any Norman College of Arms, and not being under English law they were no more subject to the jurisdiction of the English Heralds' College than either Scotland or Ireland. In the fifteenth century a pursuivant known as " Mont Orgueil Herald " existed in the College of Arms, and was possibly meant to represent the Islands, for in the British Museum is a memorandum that on January 15, 1494, £2 is granted to "Mount Orgyll pursuivant of Garnsey;" [1] but no official records made by him of insular pedigrees are known. In 1516 Randolph Jackson, then Mont Orgueil Pursuivant, was made Herald in Ordinary, but a few years later he surrendered his patent and was created Chester Herald, and the office of Mont Orgueil Herald ceased.

No heraldic visitation was ever sent to the Islands, and few families registered their arms in England, except those who acquired property and settled there.

As Payne says in his *Armorial of Jersey*,[2] the sources of the islanders' arms are "chiefly from immemorial prescription, sometimes from plagiarism, and in some instances from assumption at will." Maternal arms, especially when the mother happened to be an heiress,

[1] Colonel H. C. Carey's notes from Add. MSS. 28018, vol. ii., p. 33.
[2] P. 16.

were frequently adopted, and in some instances substituted for the paternal coat. In Jersey the de Carterets, Lemprières, and Dumaresqs, in Guernsey the families of de Sausmarez, le Marchant, and Blondel, have displayed supporters on their seals from the earliest times.

The arms of seigneuries were, in some instances, used as arms of succession, and being supposed (as in France) to go with the land, were adopted by subsequent owners of the fiefs, instead of being, like arms of office, impaled with the paternal coat.

Like the seals of the bailiwicks, the decanal seals have undergone various changes. The original seal of the Deans of Jersey was round, and bore the zodiacal sign of Pisces, with a connecting line from the mouth of each fish, and the legend, " *S. Decanatus Gersoii.*" At a later period, though still before the Reformation, the Deans used on a seal a shield bearing three bends, probably the private insignia of the ecclesiastic who first used it officially. About 1620 a larger seal was employed, of an oval shape, combining the charges of the two former seals, the fish being separated by a column, with waves in base, and in chief a shield with the three bends. Since the period of Dean Philip le Couteur, who died in 1671, the bends have been impaled with the armorial ensigns of each Dean.

The original seal of the Deans of Guernsey was a fish haurient between two croziers, surmounted by a mitre. The office of Dean, and with it the seal, was abolished at the Reformation, and not till the days of

The Channel Islands

Charles II. did the island have a Protestant Dean in the person of John de Sausmarez.

Charles sent over a new seal, vesica-shaped, representing a church (? St. Peter-Port), with a crowned King seated in front of it. In 1852 the then Bishop of Winchester (Sumner) gave this seal away, and sent a new and totally incorrect one in its place. However, thanks to the late Sir Edgar MacCulloch, the old seal was restored to the Deanery, and is still used.

Each island flies a separate flag; Jersey having adopted the red saltire of St. Patrick, while Guernsey flies the banner of St. George.

LA COTTE, ST. BRELADE, JERSEY.

CHAPTER V

BATTLE, MURDER, AND SUDDEN DEATH

In the two hundred and eighty years that elapsed between the separation from Normandy in 1204 and the Treaty of Neutrality in 1484, the Islands experienced successive invasions by the French, attacks that were repelled, though with varying success, by the gallantry of the inhabitants, but which always involved much loss of life and property; for, as Mr. Nicolle has pointed out in his article on " Le Victorial," [1] during that part of the Middle Ages when England held Aquitaine and Gascony, these Islands formed an invaluable naval base, and naturally became the centre on which French efforts were focussed. As de Roches, then Warden (1328), wrote, these Islands were "the particular part of the world the French most covet, for if they had them they intend to be lords of the sea." Yet the Islanders were but ill-provided to defend themselves against so formidable a foe; their castles were in bad repair, poorly armed and feebly manned, and their towns and harbours lay open to attack. In 1275 Edward I. ordered a jetty between St. Peter-Port and Castle Cornet to be built, the cost to be defrayed by a duty of twelve sols on all ships and six sols on all boats arriving in the island. This jetty

[1] *Bulletin Société Jersiaise*, 1923.

was the nucleus of the Guernsey harbour, afterwards the source of the island's commercial prosperity. But this bulwark was then but of little avail, as—according to a petition of 1294—the Islanders had again experienced another invasion, in which about 1,500 inhabitants were killed, houses and corn burnt, and the churches desecrated and spoiled. Edward II. having married a French Princess, peace endured during the twenty years (1307-27) of his reign; but this alliance led to the Crown of France being claimed by his son, Edward III., and the Hundred Years' War was the consequence.

From the outbreak of hostilities in 1337 there had been a good deal of fighting at sea, and the Normans formed the idea of a new Conquest of England, which, although not destined to materialise, yet was so far successful that Southampton was raided and burnt and the Channel Islands were occupied. For the French had equipped the strongest fleet which had hitherto ever been seen in the Channel, and Admiral Béhuchet invaded Jersey, where, though Mont Orgueil, with its garrison of Jerseymen, successfully defied the foe, the island was raided and burnt. Guernsey was captured *en bloc* for lack of foresight on part of the Governor, Thomas de Ferrars, as we are told in the Précepte d'Assize, and it was not until the naval victory of Sluys in October 1340, that the French were forced to abandon the island, although they retained possession of Castle Cornet until 1345, when Edward III. sent over a strong force to assist the islanders in expelling the enemy. In the

Battle, Murder, and Sudden Death

accounts of Thomas de Ferrers, then Warden of the Islands, is a note of the wages paid to thirty-one seamen employed in a barge to sail round the castle and prevent supplies being brought from Normandy to the garrison, from August 1 to September 29, 1342, showing that the principles of " blockade " were even then understood. St. Peter-Port, which had now been laid waste for the third time in sixty years, was, in 1350, by the King's orders, enclosed by a wall, as the Castle of Jerbourg, hitherto used as a place of refuge, had also been destroyed. But again the war-cry of " *Diex aïe* "—that appeal for help and succour to the Christian God of Battles which had succeeded the old Norse appeal to " Thor "—echoed through the land, and, in 1356, Castle Cornet was again in the hands of the French. It was successfully relieved by a force from Jersey, and an incident in this campaign throws light on the insular politics of that date.[1]

During the siege the Jerseymen executed, on a charge of treason, a leading Guernseyman called William le Feyvre, who had married Colette de Sausmarez, daughter of the Seigneur of Sausmarez. His widow instituted proceedings in the Guernsey Court, but the King ordered the proceedings to be stopped. On this she appealed to His Majesty, claiming that at the time of his death " her husband was under the King's special protection " and had been done to death by the Jerseymen " out of ancient enmity and their own malice." The King then ordered an enquiry; at the trial the Jerseymen were

[1] *Mont Orgueil Castle*, by E. Toulmin Nicolle, pp. 17-18.

found guilty and banished, but Sir Reginald de Cartere
and Ralph Lemprière, who had taken part in the siege
and were present in Court, challenged the verdict, saying
that the responsibility lay as much with them as with
those who had been condemned; and in consequence
they also were imprisoned in Castle Cornet. On this
the inter-insular feud—always latent—broke out in full
force. John le Marchant, Bailiff of Guernsey, and the
jurats wrote to the chancellor of England complaining
that the "bon et lèal" Otho de Holland was to be
replaced as governor of the Islands by Edmund de
Chesney, eldest son and heir of Sir William de Chesney
Seigneur of Fief le Comte. This Edmund was, they
said, in league with these Jersey miscreants, and would
therefore allow them to go unpunished. Consequently
rather than be ruled by such a governor, they would
prefer to renounce their lands and seek refuge in
England. Notwithstanding these protests, de Holland
was superseded by Edmund de Chesney in January
1359, and two months later de Carteret and Lemprière
were pardoned by the King by reason of their service
in recovering the castle, and of the fact that they were
not present at the execution. Meanwhile Edmund de
Chesney's sister, Joan, married John le Marchant's son
Denis, and, presumably, all was forgiven and forgotten
while the short interval of peace was devoted to building, for the further protection of St. Peter-Port, the
Castle of Beauregard which stood on the height commanding the southern boundary of the town.

In 1372 yet another invasion of Guernsey took place

MONT ORGUEIL CASTLE, JERSEY.

it is known in local prose and rhyme as "La Descente des Aragousais." The invading host was furnished by Charles V. of France, reinforced by Spanish mercenaries, and led by Evan (or Owen), a grand-nephew of the last independent Prince of Wales, who landed at Vazon Bay and marched across the island, finally defeating the Guernseymen in a pitched battle on the plateau west of St. Peter-Port. According to a contemporary French chronicler,[1] "Et sachiez que jeunes femmes et les boiselettes des dictes ysles avoient en ce printemps de lors fait chapeaulx de fleurs et de violettes et les avoient donnez aux jeunez hommes, et leur disoient que cil se devoient bien deffendre qui les avoient à amies." A local ballad, the only one of historic importance and of a date previous to the introduction of printing which has survived, gives an account of this invasion and subsequent battle, saying how

> " C'étoit pitié cette journée
> D'ouïr les pleurs de l'assemblée
> Des dames de St. Pierre Port."

Edmund Rose the Governor and the remnants of his army retreated into Castle Cornet, and, after vainly endeavouring to subdue this last resort, the enemy sailed away.

In consequence of this new danger the inhabitants of Jersey appealed to England for protection, and their fears were well founded, for in the following year—

[1] *Chronique des Quatre Premiers Valois*, edited by S. Luce, pp. 230-1.

The Channel Islands

July 1373—the French fleet, commanded by the famous Bertrand du Guesclin, ravaged their island and laid siege to Mont Orgueil, but was successfully repulsed by the islanders, who thus established their claim to the honour of being the only portion of the Crown possessions which had successfully opposed the greatest French General of the Middle Ages. Again, in 1406, the French returned to the fray, under the command of Pierre de Pontbriand, a Breton knight, who was accompanied by Pedro Nino, a young Castilian grandee, and a mixed force of Normans, Bretons, and Spaniards; after two fierce battles the islanders only escaped utter destruction by payment of a large ransom.

Meanwhile the unfortunate Islanders were not only devastated by incessant warfare, but were grievously affected by the great schism which had split asunder the one stable element in Europe—the great Catholic Church—to whom all Western Europe owed allegiance. For the Church was then divided into two factions—one owing obedience to the Pope at Rome, the other to the Pope at Avignon. The Channel Islands were then in the paradoxical situation that, although politically separated from Normandy in 1204, yet ecclesiastically they were still in the Norman diocese of Coutances. This situation had been accepted by the Kings of England, who still hoped to recover their ancient Duchy, and, while English Kings and Norman Bishops both owed allegiance to the Pope of Rome, it did not really so much matter; therefore, up to 1382, we find that, although their respective countries were continually at war, the Norman clergy in the Islands were practically unmolested. But now the bond of union between Church and State was rudely snapped asunder, for from 1378 until 1409 France, Scotland, and Castille would only recognise the Pope at Avignon, while the rest of Europe, including England, would only recognise the Pope at Rome. The Bishop of Coutances, with the other French clergy, pinned his faith to Clement VII. at Avignon, and his diocese, including the Channel Islands, naturally sided with him. The consequence was that, in 1382, King Richard II. issued Royal letters to the Deans of Jersey and Guernsey "Adherents to the Antipope" forbidding them to hold ecclesiastical Courts in their respective Deaneries.

Henry IV., Richard's successor, by way of detaching the Islands still further from Coutances, obtained a Bull from Boniface IX., the new Pope of Rome, transferring the Islands to the spiritual jurisdiction of Pierre, Bishop of Nantes, who was, incidentally, an adherent of the English cause in France. Although after the Council of Constance—when France shook off her allegiance to the Pope at Avignon and returned to the obedience of Rome—the Islands were restored to the diocese of Coutances, yet the bonds between the English Crown and the Norman clergy were sensibly weakened, and, in 1413, the statute of Henry V. confiscating the alien priories in the Islands was issued. Two years later Henry won the Battle of Agincourt and soon completed the conquest of the whole of Normandy, with the exception of the famous Abbey-fortress of Mont St.

Michel, which held out for its rightful King for upwards of thirty years. In the year 1425 a determined effort to capture it was made by England, and all the "free ports" of the kingdom—of which Guernsey was one—contributed ships and men for the purpose. The Guernsey contingent consisted of three ships, *La Pitié*, *La Marie*, and *La Trinité*, commanded respectively by Denis le Marchant, Pierre Nicholas, and Edmond Henry, all jurats of the Royal Court, who had under them twenty-nine men-at-arms and eighty-nine archers and sailors.[1] In recompense for these and similar services, on the 8th of May, 1444, Henry VI. issued Letters Patent to the towns of Plymouth, Poole, Dartmouth, and Southampton, stating that, as Guernsey was a "free port," she was therefore exempt from all tolls, dues, etc., on her merchandise, and from "petite coûtume," in English ports, towns, and harbours, this being a corroboration of an earlier Charter of Richard II., dated 1394, by which all the Islands had been exempted from all "tolls, exactions and dues." Meanwhile various Jerseymen who had taken part in the campaigns in Normandy of Henry V.—John de St. Martin, John Lemprière, and Ralph Tourgis amongst them—were rewarded by the King by grants of forfeited manors in that province.

On the death of Henry V. England was torn asunder by the Wars of the Roses, for Edward of York (afterwards Edward IV.) and Henry of Lancaster (Henry VI.)

[1] *Chronique de Mont St. Michel*, edited by Siméon Luce, t. i., p. 192.

both claimed to be rightful heirs, and alternately occupied the throne. In these wars the Islands were deeply involved.

In the fifteenth century the Kings of England reverted to the original tenure in fief of the Islands which had been inaugurated by King John, in 1200, by his gift of them to Pierre de Préaux. Thus, in 1415 Henry V. gave these Islands to his brother, John, Duke of Bedford. Bedford was succeeded by another brother, Humphrey, Duke of Gloucester. As both of these royal brothers died childless, the Islands reverted to the Crown, and Henry VI. granted them to his old friend Henry de Beauchamp, Duke of Warwick, with remainder to his heirs, for the symbolic yearly rent of a red rose. Warwick's only child, Anne, having died young, his sister Anne became his heiress. She had married Henry Neville, first cousin of the Duke of York, the famous "King-maker," who, in her right, thus became Earl of Warwick and "Seigneur des Isles."

As is well known, Warwick was, until just before his death, the head of the "White Rose" or Yorkist Party, and, in 1451, he and his army were marching on London. Fearing that the Yorkists would instigate a French invasion of England under cover of the Channel Islands, Henry VI., in 1452, though evidently afraid to take the Islands away from Warwick, yet appointed his faithful ally, John Nanfan, as Captain and Governor under him, evidently both to act as a check and to win adherents to the Lancastrian cause. In 1461, after the Yorkist victory of Towton, which established Edward

The Channel Islands

of York on the throne and made Henry VI. a prisoner,
it is said that Henry's Queen, Margaret of Anjou, and
her son, took refuge in Nanfan's Worcestershire Manor
of Birtsmorton Court. Driven to desperation, Margaret went so far as to sell the Channel Islands to her
own first cousin, Pierre de Brezé, Comte de Maulévrier,
Seneschal of Normandy, "pour en jouïr, lui et sa
posterité, à jamais, sans relever de la Couronne d'Angleterre," in return for his support against her husband's
enemies. De Brezé sent his cousin Carbonnel, Seigneur
de Surdeval, over to Jersey, where he and his men were
treacherously brought into Mont Orgueil Castle by "ce
faulx traistre" (as the Jerseymen called him) Guillaume
de St. Martin, and there Nanfan, the Governor, was
found to be conveniently asleep. Thus the French,
who had unsuccessfully attempted to capture Guernsey
en route, were, by treachery, enabled to get possession
of Jersey, which they held for seven long years.

A French document [1] which has recently come to
light relates how Warwick—then at Calais—sent over
an incompetent Englishman, called John Hareford, to
spy out the land. He was promptly captured, and
thereupon turned traitor and was used by Carbonnel to
gain the confidence of the Islanders—which he afterwards betrayed—as to the local conspiracy, led by
Reginald Lemprière, Seigneur de Rosel, and by Philip

[1] MS. de Chantilly (No. 1340). " Une Enquête fait au Château
du Mont Orgueil par Guillaume Carbonnel, Lt. du Comte de
Maulévrier, au sujet des menées d'un prisonnier Anglais nommé
Jehan Hareford. Dec. 1463."

86

Battle, Murder, and Sudden Death

de Carteret, Seigneur de St. Ouen, to get into touch with Yorkist sympathisers in Guernsey, and thus raise a force to drive the French out of the island.

According to this document both Lemprière and de Carteret were outwardly on such friendly terms with Carbonnel that they and their wives dined with him at Mont Orgueil, and he played tennis—" le jeu de paume "—at Rosel and dined at the Manor of St. Ouen, yet underneath the mask smouldered the undying insular hostility to French rule. Lemprière was made a prisoner, and was killed or executed at Mont Orgueil before 1468, when it was relieved by an English and insular force under the command of the Yorkist leader, Richard Harliston. For de Carteret had come in touch with Harliston. Under cover of night the people invested the castle, and dawn showed the garrison that they were surrounded by the English on the sea and by Jerseymen on the land. Edward IV., recognising the great assistance the Jersey Militia had rendered in this relief, issued Letters Patent, dated January 28, 1468-9, again exempting Jerseymen also from all tolls, customs, and subsidies payable to the Crown in the boroughs and cities of England, and further granted certain commercial privileges to John Perryn, John Tyaut, William Duport, Jordan Rogier, Thomas de Havilland, Lawrence Carey, William Mainguy, Renouf Agenor, Ralph Cousin, and Nicholas de Lisle, of Guernsey, and to Peter le Serkeés, Peter Tehy, John de Sonlemont, Nicholas le Petit, and John le Moigne, of Jersey, who had, between them, expended the then enormous sum of £2,833 6s. 8d. for the purpose of freeing Jersey from the French. Harliston's Yorkist proclivities afterwards led him to take the part of the pretender —Perkin Warbeck—who claimed to be that younger son of Edward IV. generally believed to have been murdered in the Tower by his uncle, Richard III.; and in 1485 Harliston in his turn was driven out of Mont Orgueil by an English force under Edmund de Weston, who is said to have celebrated the occasion by marrying Reginald Lemprière's widow. Warbeck may also have had sympathisers in Guernsey, for in 1482-4 Edward Brampton, a converted Portuguese Jew and Yorkist courtier, was the Governor of Guernsey, and it was as page to Brampton's wife that Warbeck learned those details of the Yorkist ménage he was afterwards to utilise so successfully.[1]

It is obvious, that while all this fighting was going on, all traffic in the Channel, whether peaceful or otherwise, was practically impossible. And yet the Islanders were dependent on the mainland not only for most of the necessities of life, but also for their spiritual needs. Therefore a mutual arrangement was made that, on payment of certain sums, the commanders of both forces could grant " safe conducts " to enemy partisans. The temptation to sell as many as possible, regardless of their destination, naturally ensued, and, undoubtedly, the abuses connected with this system were among the contributing causes which led to the famous

[1] *Perkin Warbeck and his Jewish Master*, by Cecil Roth (Jewish Historical Society, 1922).

FIQUET BAY, JERSEY.

CHAPTER VI

ECCLESIASTICAL AFFAIRS

As we have already seen, the Channel Islanders were converted to Christianity by missionaries from the Celtic Church of Wales and Brittany. These Celts were, as far as Roman Catholicism was concerned, good Christians, but bad Churchmen. For they were too mystical and too spiritual to attempt to compress the Almighty within human formulas, and the result was, that after the Synod of Whitby in 664 they followed for a time their own independent and lonely path. When the Franks overran the Armorican coasts, the Islands, already inhabited by Bretons, became a refuge to their co-religionists. It was not until the end of the eighth century that Charlemagne sent the Abbot of Fontenelle to detach the Islanders from this unorthodox influence, and they were then attached to the Neustrian —for the Normans had not yet arrived—See of Coutances. Within a few years—about A.D. 830— the tide of northern pirates began to flow over the Islands, and a hundred years later Neustria, bearing the Islands in its wake, was ceded by Charles the Simple to Rollo, the Northmen's chief; and thus it became "Normandy," and the northern "Jarl" gradually merged into the Norman "Comte," while from those days until the Reformation the Channel Islands remained attached to the Norman diocese of Coutances.

True there had been attempts made by Kings of England to synchronise their spiritual with their political allegiance: King John had attached them to the See of Exeter;[1] in 1399 Henry IV. had transferred them to the jurisdiction of the Bishop of Nantes; in 1499 Pope Alexander VI. had even gone so far as to issue a Bull transferring them to the See of Winchester. But these mandates had remained in abeyance, and, in 1542, when an open conflict occurred between King Henry VIII. and the Bishop of Coutances, Henry II. of France supported the contentions of the English Crown, and ordered the Bishop to exercise his jurisdiction in the Islands in the name of King Henry and not in that of the Pope.

Even after the Reformation the anomaly of Islands, avowedly Protestant, and for whose express benefit the Prayer Book of the Church of England had, in 1553, been translated into French, remaining in a French Roman Catholic diocese did not trouble the English Lords of Council, for, as late as April 13, 1565, on receipt of a letter from the Bishop of Coutances complaining that he had not received his ecclesiastical tithes and obits from the Islanders for seven years, they wrote to the insular authorities saying that they found his request "very reasonable" and ordering that "all such dues may, from henceforth, be paid." But, in Guernsey

[1] Assize Roll, 1309, pp. 63 and 79.

at any rate, these dues had already been appropriated by the Governor and the Dean, consequently no notice was taken of this order. Therefore, on October 26, 1565, the Bishop summoned Dean After—who had ousted his Catholic predecessor—"comme soy-disant Doyen" to produce his Commission and proofs of Canonical Institution. To this order the Dean declined to submit, claiming to have been appointed by Queen Elizabeth herself, and refused to discuss the question unless the Bishop himself renounced the Pope and all foreign jurisdiction and took the oath of allegiance to Queen Elizabeth as titular head of the Church. The Bishop, naturally enough, declined, and on this plea the Islands were, in 1568, definitely severed from Coutances and attached to the See of Winchester.

The insular Reformation may be said to have started in 1438, when Philibert de Montjeu, Bishop of Coutances, sent Franciscan monks to Jersey to repress Scottish heretics who had arrived there and were preaching "new doctrines" to the people. Two of these monks—doubtless regarded as alien spies—were stoned to death and the rest had to return from whence they came. In 1479 a special Synod assembled at Coutances to deal with the case of religious propagandists from England who were "evangelising" the Islands; and it was ordered that these heretics should be handed over to the Civil Courts for the purpose of being burnt alive.

Local records show that Roman Catholicism had but superimposed its feasts on the pagan festivals of heathen days; its churches on the sites of heathen altars; and men and women still danced round fires on St. John's Eve more in commemoration of the Solar Solstice than of the Christian Saint. In Guernsey men processed in the "Chevauchée de St. Michel" under auspices of Church and State, dancing and singing round the island, nominally to see that the ways were clear for the passage of the Host on the festival of Corpus Christi, yet nevertheless halting at pagan shrines and performing pre-Christian rites. In Jersey the Bacchanalian spring festival had been transferred to St. George's Day, April 23, and the chapel of St. George at Mont Orgueil was the rendezvous. In both islands maskings and midnight revelries abounded, and it was with great difficulty the Puritan régime of later days repressed the natural instincts of the Islanders.

At this date, however, the Islanders were still avowedly Roman Catholic; they went on pilgrimages to distant shrines, and gave their worldly goods towards Masses and obits for the redemption of their souls. Jersey, being nearer the Continent, was the first to feel the influence of Luther and of Calvin, and even made Protestant evangelisers welcome. In 1548 her Royal Court issued an order of maintenance for Martin Langloys and Thomas Johannes, who had come to proclaim the Word of God. Guernsey, on the contrary, distrustful of foreign influences, had attempted to check the Huguenot invasion by issuing, in 1534, an order against strangers coming into the island, but the expulsion of the Franciscan friars in 1537, and the preaching of a colporteur called Denis le Vair (who was subsequently burnt for heresy at Rouen in 1554) brought home to her also the strength of the religious upheaval then in progress. In 1549 King Edward VI. sent a letter to the inhabitants thanking them for their acceptance of his law regarding Divine Service; for by this time all vestiges of Catholicism—breviarys, images, and wayside crosses—had been swept away, and the Church of England was established in both islands. But, with the accession of Queen Mary in 1553, Roman Catholicism was restored and an era of persecution began. In Jersey it was comparatively mild, but in Guernsey on July 18, 1556, by order of the Bailiff—Helier Gosselin—and the Dean—Jacques Amy—three unfortunate women, Catherine Cauchés and her two daughters, were burnt for heresy, while, so far did intolerance go, that when the baby of one of the victims, born at the stake, was brought to the Bailiff, he commanded that it should be cast back into the flames. In 1558, on Queen Elizabeth's accession, Protestantism was once more established, but it was now the fierce fanaticism of Geneva, which acknowledged no authority of Bishops and Deans, but only that of Colloquies and Synods. For when the old priests were driven from their pulpits, it was to Calvin the Islanders turned to find them French-speaking substitutes. He therefore sent two of his own pupils, Morice, Seigneur de la Ripaudière, to St. Helier, and Nicholas Baudouin to St. Peter-Port. Elizabeth, with her well-known dislike of Nonconformity, hesitated to give sanction to the Presbyterian use, but Helier de Carteret of Jersey, who enjoyed her favour, pointed out that the arrival of these pastors had been a great help to them, destitute as they were of ministers of their own tongue. Nevertheless, neither the persons of these ministers nor the form of their worship was, in the first instance, popular with the Islanders. In 1564, 2,000 Guernseymen signed a petition complaining that under Dean After and Baudouin saints' days and festivals were ignored, the church services were conducted irreverently and quite contrary to the order of Queen Elizabeth's Prayer Book, that Baudouin—"the Norman" as he is contemptuously described—administered Communion without surplice or hood, silently handing the Bread and the Cup to those sitting round a table; and praying for redress. We then find that Baudouin excommunicated Nicholas Carey, Seigneur de Blanchelande, for contumacy. Carey, undaunted, appealed to Horne, Bishop of Winchester, who promptly excommunicated Baudouin, while Horne's successor, Watson, in 1580, absolved both parties from the excommunication. But, as usual, politics prevailed over piety. Evidence of Roman Catholic plots to regain the Islands showed that Catholicism stood not only for the Church but for France, for the Pope's excommunication of Elizabeth authorised Catholics to transfer their allegiance from England to Rome; while, above all, the defeat by wind and waves of that great Armada launched under auspices of Roman Pope and Catholic King to destroy Protestant England convinced the most sceptical that both God and Country were, indeed, on the Protestant side,

POINT LE GROIN, ST. BRELADE, JERSEY.

and thenceforth we find Presbyterianism firmly established in both islands. Even when officially replaced by Anglicanism—in Jersey in 1620, in Guernsey not till 1662—yet we find it lingered on in faith if not in doctrine. In Guernsey Peter de Jersey, the newly appointed Anglican Rector of St. Peter-Port, wrote to Amias Andros, the Bailiff, on August 14, 1662, that there were many who said "qu'il faut brusler Monsr. le Doyen et moy"; and in a letter dated August 26 he said: "I've not as yet used the Signe of the Crosse in Baptisme for feare of another tumult, for which cause Mr. Deane baptises on the week dayes when there is no sermon in his Parish, and, indeed, people are extreamely scandalised at it."

In Jersey, in 1755, we find the Dean obliged to resort to civil power to enforce the reading of the Litany, while a hundred years later le Quesne[1] says: "It is only of recent years that the clergy of the island have adopted the surplice; in the parish churches of Guernsey it is not worn by the clergy; no fonts are to be seen in the churches; the Communion table is usually a deal table, which is placed before the pulpit when the holy sacrament is administered; the parish clerks still read the lessons; and the rectories are still called 'Les presbytères.'" Towards the end of the eighteenth century a visit from Wesley caused a wave of Nonconformist piety to flow over the Islands, which has resulted in the number of chapels of various denominations to be found on every side.

[1] *Constitutional History of Jersey*, 1856, p. 172.

The Channel Islands

Meanwhile, besides ratifying all the Islanders' previous charters and confirming their ancient privileges, Queen Elizabeth testified her goodwill to the people of Guernsey by authorising the south arm of the old harbour to be built, and enlarging and fortifying Castle Cornet: for she knew how the Islands had incurred the enmity of the French Court by the asylum they afforded to numbers of Protestant refugees from France—including some of the highest rank—and she accordingly strengthened both Guernsey and Jersey by additional fortifications. In 1563 she granted eighty quarters of wheat rent and the lands and buildings of a convent of Franciscan Frairs or Cordeliers, who had been expelled from the island by Bailiff Compton in the reign of Henry VIII., for the foundation of a grammar school in St. Peter-Port to be called after her name. This was the precursor of the present Elizabeth College. Its first schoolmaster was Dr. Adrian Saravia, a Fleming, who afterwards proceeded to England, where, in 1600, he became one of the band of translators to whom we owe the Authorised Version of the Bible. The school for many years did not fulfil the aims of its Royal foundress. A series of incompetent and untrustworthy masters, and the apathy of the authorities, emptied it of pupils; but in 1824, after an enquiry had been made into the existing state of things, the statutes were reorganised, a new charter was granted, and the present college was built.

LE FRET POINT, JERSEY.

satisfaction, as the "ancient petitions" and the complaints to Justices of Assize abundantly prove. In the reign of Henry VII., who, while Earl of Richmond, had visited Jersey, the government of Jersey and Guernsey was definitely separated, and by a charter, dated 1494, Henry ordered that the Captain of Jersey (for it was only in 1618, by an Order in Council of James I., that these officials were awarded the title of "Governor") should possess no jurisdiction in Jersey either secular or ecclesiastical, and the nomination of both Bailiff and Dean of Jersey was in future reserved to the Crown. Nevertheless, violent altercations between Captain and Bailiff continued to take place. On one occasion Sir Hugh Vaughan, the Captain, a special protégé of Cardinal Wolsey, seeing that a case in which he, as representative of the Crown, was immediately interested was about to be decided in favour of the Islanders, drew his dagger and threatened to plunge it into the breast of the Bailiff, Helier de Carteret, should he persist in giving judgment against him. But the Channel Islander, though he can be led, will not be driven; de Carteret drew his own dagger and told the Captain that if either he or his men moved, his death would be the immediate consequence—and then pronounced judgment in favour of the insular defendant, Drouet Lemprière, who was, incidentally, his own brother-in-law. Many other trials of strength between subsequent Captains and Bailiffs supervened, until in the days of James I., by the firmness and independence with which Bailiff Herault resisted the encroachments

The Channel Islands

of Sir John Peyton, the rights of each were more clearly defined; nevertheless, the clash of interests may be said to have survived even unto our own day; and it is noteworthy that the Governor's chair in the Jersey States House is purposely made three inches lower than that of the Bailiff.

Guernsey's rights were not so clearly defined, and Sir Thomas Leighton, Captain from 1570-1609, took full advantage of the situation. Not only did he repeatedly interfere in the purely judicial procedure of the island, but he nominated as Bailiff his own nephew, Thomas Wigmore, who not only did not understand French, but is described by a contemporary as "petit homme et incapable." This appointment was, in 1601, succeeded by another still more unpopular, that of a Jerseyman, Amias de Carteret, whose nomination, whatever his abilities, was considered as a dire insult by the Guernsey people. Exasperated by this culmination of a long series of injuries, the Islanders appealed to the Crown, who, by an Order in Council of 1605, limited the Captain's jurisdiction, although the insular demand that the Crown should reserve the right of nominating Crown officials was refused, and it was not until 1674 that Charles II.—who, though an exile, and in defiance of precedent, had, in 1650, nominated Amias Andros as Bailiff of Guernsey—officially annexed that privilege.

It was inevitable that the division of the governments should begin the separation of the interests of the Islands, and this separation was intensified in the wars of the seventeenth century between King and Parliament. In Jersey, Philip de Carteret, Seigneur de St. Ouen, was virtual ruler. He combined the offices of Lieutenant-Governor and Bailiff, and thus practically monopolised the military and civil authority of the island. As Lieutenant-Governor his official residence was Mont Orgueil, and while there he had the custody of William Prynne, the barrister, whose *Histrio-Mastyx* had given so much offence at the Court of Charles I., and who, after having been branded and losing his ears, had been banished to Jersey in 1637 by Charles and the Star Chamber. Sir Philip treated his captive with great kindness and consideration, and allowed him every indulgence in his power, while the ladies of his household did their best to ameliorate the three years' imprisonment of their captive.

Sir Philip had to pay the usual penalty of success by exciting the hostility and jealousy of a number of his fellow-citizens, notably Dean Bandinel and Michael Lemprière, who, because Sir Philip had espoused the cause of the Stuarts, immediately took the side of the Parliament. These enemies took advantage of the political circumstances of the period to forward a series of accusations against Sir Philip to the English Parliament. These machinations were, however, defeated by Prynne, who boldly and openly championed his quondam gaoler. This conduct was violently assailed by the Jersey malcontents in a pamphlet called *Pseudo-Mastyx*. Thus the island was divided into two factions, the Royalists under de Carteret being known as the "Bien affectionnés" and the Republicans under Bandinel and Lemprière as the "Réfractaires." The feeling between the parties became so bitter that in 1643 Philip found himself besieged in Elizabeth Castle, while his wife (Anne, daughter of Sir Francis Dowse) and Philip, his eldest son, were in the same condition at Mont Orgueil. After many privations, and while still in a state of siege, he fell ill in the autumn of the same year, neither his wife nor his mother being allowed access to him until he was at the point of death. His widow and son continued to hold Mont Orgueil against the foe until Captain George Carteret[1] came to the island to take up the post of Lieutenant-Governor, and caused the siege to be raised and the Parliamentarian party to flee. This George Carteret was both nephew and son-in-law of Sir Philip, having married Elizabeth, his youngest daughter. Being in the Royal Navy, he proceeded to fit out privateers, duly authorised by letters of marque, which, by capturing richly laden vessels of the Parliamentarians, did much harm to the enemy and supplied money to advance the Royal cause. To legalise these proceedings Charles I., on December 13, 1644, made Captain Carteret Vice-Admiral of the Fleet, and thus his *pataches* acquired the dignity of men-of-war.

The new Admiral did not forget the injuries inflicted by the opposite party on his predecessor, and in 1644 the Bandinels, father and son, were arrested and imprisoned in Mont Orgueil. After fourteen months' imprisonment, they concocted a plan of escape: they

---

[1] He thus wrote his name, dropping the particle.

knotted their bedclothes into a rope, and on a dark, tempestuous night crept through a narrow window over-looking the steep rocks which encircled the castle. But they had miscalculated the distance, and both fell bruised and maimed on the rocks, and died from the injuries thus received.

In 1629 Jersey and Guernsey were visited by the Rev. Peter Heylyn, who came over in the suite of Lord Danby, and his description of them, entitled *A Survey of the Estate of Guernzey and Jarsey*, printed in 1656, is one of the earliest authentic accounts of the Islands we possess. He describes the country folk of Jersey as "a people very painfull and laborious; but by reason of their continuall toyle and labour, not a little affected by a kinde of melancholy surlinesse incident to plough-men." He also notices the great poverty of the majority of the inhabitants. He describes Jersey as "generally swelling up in pretty hillocks, under which lie pleasant Vallies, and those plentifully watered with dainty Rils or Riverets, in which watery commodity it hath ques-tionlesse the precedency of Guernzey. Both Islands consist very much of small Inclosures, every man in each of them having somewhat to live on of his own, only the difference is that here the Mounds are made with ditches and banks of earth cast up, well fenced and planted with several sorts of apples, out of which they make a pleasing kinde of Sider, which is their ordinary drink; whereas in Guernzey they are for the most part made of stones, about the height and fashion of a Parapet."

The Channel Islands

To this island of "pretty hillocks and pleasant Vallies" Charles I., for safety's sake, determined to send the Prince of Wales; and on April 17, 1646, Prince Charles, on board the *Proud Black Eagle*, commanded by Captain Baldwin Wake, and attended by a large suite—including Sir Edward Hyde (afterwards Lord Clarendon), Mr. Lane, Sir Richard Fanshaw, and many others—cast anchor before Elizabeth Castle. Great were the rejoicings on the island at this signal manifestation of Royal confidence.

Soon after the Prince's arrival Sir George Carteret, who had recently been created a baronet, ordered the Militia to assemble on a spot in St. Aubin's Bay for a great review.

On June 27, 1646, by the direction of his parents, Charles left Jersey to join his mother at Fontainebleau. He had charmed the Islanders by his *bonhomie* and simplicity, as well as by the grace and elegance of his bearing. " C'étoit un Prince grandement bénin," wrote Chevalier; and already he exercised that fatal fascination, which, in spite of all their innate falsity, seems to have been the special attribute of most of the Stuarts.

While he was in France, Charles, at the instigation of the Governor, Sir Thomas Jermyn, started negotiations with regard to the sale of the Channel Islands. But two obstacles stood in the way. Guernsey was as staunchly Parliamentary as Jersey was Royalist, and would have required to be captured by a special force, which it was impossible to raise at that juncture; and Sir George Carteret, Lord Capel, Sir Edward Hyde, and

Sixteenth and Seventeenth Centuries

Sir Ralph Hopton, hearing of these proposals, signed a deed on October 19, 1646, by which they bound themselves to deliver up the island to the Parliamentarians should France accept Charles's offer; the matter therefore was of necessity dropped.

Lord Clarendon did not accompany his master to France, but remained in Jersey at Elizabeth Castle, and there compiled the greater part of his *History of the Rebellion*.

At the time of the execution of Charles I. Jersey was almost the only stronghold in the kingdom that still continued loyal to the Stuarts, and there on February 17, 1649, Charles II. was proclaimed King with much rejoicing.

In September 1649 Charles, with the Duke of York and three hundred followers, returned to Jersey, and took up his abode in his old quarters at Elizabeth Castle. This visit seems to have been spent in nothing but a round of semi-state entertainments and local festivities. The Sunday following his arrival Charles attended service at the old parish church of St. Helier in great state, clad entirely in purple, and with a purple scarf across his breast, while the church was decorated with green boughs and flowers, and the aisle strewed with rushes.

During this second visit to the island, Charles's popularity was greater than ever. He frequently visited the local gentry at their houses, and joined in their shooting parties, the game in those days consisting of hares, rabbits, and red-legged partridges—a species which, though now extinct in the Islands, was at that time plentiful there. One of his first acts was to stand sponsor to Sir George Carteret's infant daughter, whom he named Caroline, after himself. He also touched eleven persons for "King's Evil," and hung, as Chevalier tells us, "un angelot avec un ruban blanc" round their necks.

Shortly before his departure, which took place in February, 1650, Charles held a Court at Elizabeth Castle. On this occasion the local authorities and principal gentry kissed His Majesty's hand, and the holders of "francs fiefs nobles" did homage. According to Pirouet, another old Jersey diarist, Charles "y convia toutes les nobles demoiselles de Jersey, avec plusieurs gentilshommes, et le Roy y fit le choix d'une femme pour le Seigneur de S. Ouen, nommée Ann Dumaresq de la Maison des Augrès." These ceremonies flattered the self-esteem of the Islanders, who apparently did not realise that they were paying for them out of their own pockets, as the greater part of Charles's revenues during this second visit were again drawn from the coffers of Sir George Carteret and the Jersey people.

Almost immediately after the Battle of Worcester, Colonel Haines and a large body of troops embarked on board a fleet of eighty ships, commanded by the redoubtable Blake, and on October 20, 1651, they attacked Jersey. On October 27 St. Aubin's Fort and Mont Orgueil Castle surrendered, and seven weeks later Elizabeth Castle, under the command of Sir George Carteret, blockaded by sea and besieged by land, was

ELIZABETH CASTLE, JERSEY.

forced to follow their example, though upon the most favourable terms, the garrison marching out with their horses and arms, colours flying, drums beating, and all the honours of war; and for the next nine years the island groaned under the iron rule of the Parliamentarians.

Sir George went to France and joined the King, and did not return to England until he rode with Charles on his triumphal entry into London, May 29, 1660.

In order to testify his gratitude for the signal services he had received at the hands of the Jersey people, Charles caused a silver-gilt mace to be made and presented to the civil authorities of the island, and this is still kept at the Royal Court and carried before the Bailiff and magistrates on state occasions.

In the early part of 1659, the King had given to Sir George Carteret[1] "a certain island and adjacent islets near Virginia in America, in perpetual inheritance." To those islands the name of New Jersey was given, and the King's Patent granted permission " to build towns, churches, and castles, and to establish suitable laws, and also power to transport thither three hundred persons for the purpose of cultivating the land." In 1665 Philip de Carteret, Seigneur of La Hougue—a distant cousin of Sir George—received a commission as Governor of this Province, and he landed at Elizabeth Port, which he so named after Elizabeth, wife of Sir George, and

---

[1] At Sir George's death in 1679 his American possessions were offered for sale, and in February 1682 they were bought for £3,400 by William Penn and his eleven Quaker associates.

daughter of Sir Philip de Carteret. And it was during his stay in America that Philip de Carteret had so many disputes with his autocratic cousin, Sir Edmund Andros, Governor of New York.[1]

After the Restoration, Charles heaped honours and titles upon the de Carterets.

Local tradition has coupled the names of Charles II. and Marguerite de Carteret, daughter of the Seigneur of Trinity. In the first edition of this book the author, following the lead of the late Lord Acton, assumed the genuineness of certain letters purporting to be written by Charles II. to the General of the Jesuits in Rome. These letters claimed that a certain James de la Cloche " of Jersey " was his eldest son, " born to Us when we were not more than 16 or 17 years of age of a young lady of a family amongst the most distinguished in our kingdom," and might, " under certain eventualities even entertain hopes of arriving to the Crown." On these letters, therefore, the author assumed that la Cloche was not only the son of Charles and Marguerite de Carteret, but possibly also the mysterious prisoner known as the " Man in the Iron Mask." This theory as to his parentage was so honoured by Monsignor A. S. Barnes that he adopted it as his own in his *The Man of the Mask*, published in 1910, six years after the appearance of the *Channel Islands*. But, in a subsequent edition, published 1912, Monsignor Barnes claims to have " been able to prove, in conjunction with Mr. Andrew Lang,

[1] Son of Thomas Andros, Seigneur of Sausmarez in Guernsey, and Elizabeth, daughter of Amias de Carteret, Bailiff of Guernsey.

that these letters were all forgeries." Consequently the whole theory necessarily falls to the ground, and Marguerite de Carteret's reputation is cleared for all time.

Meanwhile the seventeenth century, which had brought prosperity to Jersey, reduced the people of Guernsey to a state of great discontent and distress.

Charles I. had destroyed the tobacco crops whereby they had hoped to increase their fortunes, and, like his predecessor, had sent over successive garrisons of soldiers, the entire cost of which, contrary to law and justice, the Islanders were made to defray. A petition dated September 29, 1629, sets forth that the island was then visited with a great plague, "whereby all commerce is taken from us, and all manner of imployment both in towne and countrey, and that the inhabitants are growne exceedinge poore, what with the losse of almost all theire shippinge during the laste troubles with Fraunce, as also with taxes for fortiffications and enterteienment of the soldiers, insoemuch that the best abel can hardly supplie theire owne necessities, the other being like to perish for want."[1] In spite of petitions and deputations, however, the Islanders failed to recover any of the money they were thus forced to disburse. Nevertheless, when in 1636 a large Guernsey vessel homeward bound from Newfoundland was taken captive and its island crew sold into slavery by Algerian pirates, the Royal Court prayed the King to ransom the prisoners, adding that should he consent to do so the

[1] Actes des États, i., p. 156.

Islanders would then acquit him of all arrears of debt.[1] To this request, as to all that had preceded it, the King turned a deaf ear, so that it is not to be wondered at that the majority of Guernseymen took the side of the Parliament in the ensuing Civil War.

Furthermore, the religious as well as the political bias of the Guernsey people was on the side of the Protestant and devout Cromwellians and opposed to the wild and graceless Cavaliers, though a certain minority, including Sir Henry de Vic, the Androses of Sausmarez, Jacques Guille of St. George, and Peter Priaulx of Le Comte, remained loyal to the Crown. Also, as Dr. Latham points out,[2] personal influence in both islands had much to do with the matter : the de Carterets imposed Royalist feelings on Jersey; "the Parliamentarian feeling of the Guernseymen seems to have been determined by the Careys, de Beauvoirs, and similar influential families."

In 1643 an order came from the Parliamentary Commissioners to the island authorities bidding them apprehend Sir Peter Osborne, the Lieutenant-Governor, seize all the fortresses in Guernsey and the Bailiwick, and hold the island for the Parliament. Thereupon Sir Peter retired to his official residence of Castle Cornet, which in those days was an island and inaccessible from the town except at the very lowest tides, and, with Mr. Amias Andros and a small handful of troops, entrenched himself against the foe, and on March 11, 1643-4, the siege of Castle Cornet began.

---

[1] Actes des États, i., pp. 175-6.
[2] *Channel Islands*, 1st edition, p. 393.

Sixteenth and Seventeenth Centuries

Peter de Beauvoir, Seigneur des Granges, Peter Carey,[1] and James de Havilland were at this date appointed Parliamentary Commissioners for Guernsey, and on October 21 they were fraudulently induced by a Royalist emissary called Bowden to go on board his ship, the *George*, on the pretext of there discussing affairs of the highest importance. No sooner had they set foot on the vessel than they found themselves prisoners, and Bowden delivered them into the hands of Sir Peter Osborne, who incarcerated them "in one of the deepest dungeons under the lower ditch—a place so subterranean and humid that our hair became wet, and from thence we were unable to see light but through the keyhole."[2]

After some weeks of misery the prisoners were moved into an upper dungeon which had a window, and there they began to cut a hole through the floor with their knives, and so were enabled, by means of a hook they had secured, to obtain some old cotton match in the room beneath. This cotton they twisted into three ropes, and by this means, on Sunday, December 3, they lowered themselves through the window and down the

[1] Peter de Beauvoir and Peter Carey were first cousins, being sons respectively of Judith and Marie Germain, and through their common grandmother—Anne le Moyne, wife of Gilles Germain—descended from Breton Protestant refugees. Peter Carey was, moreover, paternally descended from Jaquine Lefebvre, the daughter of an exiled Huguenot Seigneur of Vitré. Peter de Beauvoir married, as his first wife, his cousin, Jeanne le Moyne. The Huguenot connection doubtless had great influence in these two cases.

[2] Peter Carey's Diary.

walls on to the rocks beneath. They ran along the western beach, it being low water at the time, without attracting notice; and although they were seen and fired upon the moment they left the cover of the walls and made for the town, they ultimately succeeded in reaching the steps of the South Pier unhurt. The news being carried to the town church, where service was proceeding, the whole congregation rushed out to welcome them, and the bells rang out the tidings of their deliverance. It was discovered afterwards that had the prisoners postponed their escape for half an hour they would assuredly have been hanged, as an order to that effect had just arrived from the King. The English Parliamentary chronicle, entitled *God's Arke Overtopping the World's Waves*, contained in January, 1644, an account of this event, and described how " Mounsieur le Grande, Mounsieur Carey, and Mounsieur Haverly, three faithfull and fast friends to the Parliament," had been treacherously betrayed into the hands of " that perfidious viper of his native countrey, Sir Peter Osborn "; and gave the manner of their escape and their joyous reception at the hands of the Guernsey people, " they being three of the most prudent and pious protectors of the welfare of that island."

As we have already seen, the little garrison of Castle Cornet still continued to make a gallant resistance. Sir Peter Osborne was replaced by Sir Baldwin Wake, Sir Baldwin by Colonel Burgess; but each commander and his men equally remained loyal to their trust, although by this time the King's party had been weakened and worsted, and the King himself captured, imprisoned, and put to death. The supplies with which Sir George Carteret and the Royalist party in Jersey endeavoured to succour them were frequently cut off by hostile vessels. Often and often the garrison were in a state of semi-starvation, being generally limited to one meal a day, eked out with limpets and hake which they caught off the rocks, and which, for lack of oil or lard, they were fain to fry in the tallow used for greasing the cannons. And while they were enduring these privations they were forced to be constantly on the alert, for at all states of the tide, and both by night and day, Parliamentary men-of-war and island enemies attempted to take the castle unawares.

The state of the townspeople must equally have been one of great misery, continually exposed as they were to the fire of the castle's cannon, from which Pierre le Roy[1] tells us more than thirty thousand shots had been fired into the town; and de la Marche, another contemporary diarist, after referring to a storm which had destroyed a large portion of the harbour, goes on to tell how Sir Peter Osborne with his great guns had made a much greater breach in St. Peter-Port than that which the storm had made in the pier. In those days the houses of almost all the gentlefolk of the island were situated in St. Peter-Port, which was still surrounded

---

[1] Pierre le Roy was a Guernsey schoolmaster in the days of the Stuarts. His notebook still survives, and was edited and translated by the Rev. G. E. Lee, M.A., F.S.A., for the Guernsey Historical and Antiquarian Society in 1893.

by its old walls pierced by their various gates, and flanked on the south by the ruins of the Tour de Beauregard and on the north by the Tour Gand. This northern end of the town being especially exposed to the guns of Castle Cornet, the Court removed from the Plaiderie to Elizabeth College, then on a lower and less prominent site than it occupies at present.

When the siege of Castle Cornet had lasted for eight years and nine months, Cromwell, exasperated at this protracted resistance, despatched a strong force under Admiral Blake to subdue it as well as the equally contumacious island of Jersey. After the surrender of Elizabeth Castle, Castle Cornet was surrounded, and the garrison, being reduced to great straits, were at last obliged to capitulate. They had gained, however, the proud distinction of being the last fortress in the British Islands to yield to the authority of the Parliament. On December 19, 1651, Colonel Burgess and his valiant company left their prison walls, having received permission to march forth with " their arms and all their wearing apparel of whatsoever kind, drums beating, ensigns displayed, bullet in mouth, and match lighted at both ends, into the island of Guernsey, there to lay down all their arms, except their swords, and those they shall be permitted to wear, enjoy, and take away," and with an indemnity of £1,500 sterling.[1]

Charles II., after his restoration, seems to have treated his quondam foes with great magnanimity, and ordered

[1] " Articles of Capitulation for the Surrender of Castle Cornet," *Chronicles*, p. 319.

a general pardon, from which, however, five persons were declared exempt—namely, Sir Henry de Vic,[1] knight and baronet, Messrs. Amias, Edmund, and Charles Andros, and Mr. Nathaniel Darell,[2] who, "having con-

---

[1] A scion of a very old Guernsey family, members of which had been rectors of island livings or jurats of the Royal Court from the thirteenth and fourteenth centuries. Sir Henry was a son of John de Vic, the King's Procureur, and Elizabeth Pageot, a Guernsey woman. All English biographers of de Vic, including Burke (*Extinct Baronetcies*), Le Neve, and the Westminster Abbey Registers, state that "Sir Henry's mother appears to have been Rachel, eldest daughter of Sir Philip Carteret (*sic*), and that he married his cousin Margaret"; but this statement is entirely without foundation. The St. Peter-Port Registers prove that he was the son of his father's second wife Elizabeth Pageot, and was baptised on November 23, 1597. Her relations settled in England and acquired wealth, their name being anglicised to Paget, and it is supposed that it was due to their influence that Sir Henry owed his advancement in life. He became French secretary to Charles I. in 1635, was knighted in 1641 while British Resident at Brussels, and shared in the exile of Charles II., who created him a baronet in 1649. He was subsequently Comptroller of the Household to the Duke of York, and Chancellor of the Order of the Garter, he and Sir William Cecil (in the reign of Edward VI.) being the only two laymen who have ever filled that honourable station. He married Margaret de Carteret, daughter of the Sir Philip de Carteret mentioned as being Prynne's gaoler in Mont Orgueil; and his daughter, Lady Frescheville—noted, according to Pepys, for her dancing—was lady-in-waiting to Queen Anne. Sir Henry died in 1671, and was buried in Westminster Abbey.

[2] Nathaniel Darell, a Captain in the Army and Lieutenant-Governor of Guernsey, married an Islander, Anne de Beauvoir, widow of Thomas le Marchant, and sister of the Peter de Beauvoir who was imprisoned with Peter Carey and James de Havilland in Castle Cornet.

tinued inviolably faithful to His Majesty," had no need
to be included.

On the death of the first Lord Hatton in 1670, his
son succeeded him in the government of Guernsey as
well as in the title, and took up his residence, as every
previous Governor had done, at Castle Cornet, his house
being situated just below the old tower which formerly
surmounted the Castle. He had resided there for two
years when, on December 29, 1672, a dreadful calamity
befell him, of which a contemporary account is preserved
by his descendants.[1]

In his youth the " wise woman of Rockingham " had
given him the following warning :

> " Kit Hatton ! Kit Hatton ! I rede ye beware
> Of the flash from the cloud and the flight through the air !
> When the star of thy destiny looms in the sky,
> To others unclouded, but red to thine eye,
> Though men see no signs in the threatening air—
> Kit Hatton ! Kit Hatton ! I rede ye beware !"

The family manuscript relates that on this December
night Lord Hatton being with Ensign Covett, the latter
said, " ' Pray, observe that starr,' and his lordship, looking earnestly at it, said, ' It looks very angry; I wish
we have not some foul weather.' But to the informant's
judgment he never saw a clearer skye." And at one
o'clock next morning, which was New Year's Day,
Chapple was awakened by a fellow-servant who told

[1] This account is given in an article in *Blackwood's Magazine* for
1873 (pp. 476 *et seq.*), written by Lord Winchilsea, one of the
descendants of the hero of this tragedy, and taken from the original
deposition of James Chapple, an eyewitness of the event.

him "he did believe the house was falling," and when they got out he "heard his lord's voice calling for help," and found Lord Hatton on the Castle wall "with the mattress and feather-bed under him, and the bed-clothes over him"; and carried his lordship into the guardroom, and went down into the castle "to see for his lordship's lady, mother, and sisters, and then found that the castle was blown up, and the dowager lady dead in her bed, being posted on the head with a great stone." And in the next apartment his two sisters were both alive in bed, "but almost suffocated with a beam of the house fallen betwixt them." On digging among the ruins they successfully extricated Miss Anne Hatton,[1] then three years old; in another bed they found one of the nurses dead, with Miss Margaret Hatton, a child of eighteen months old, "in her arms, playing with a little silver cup in its hand," and the baby of three weeks old, Elizabeth Hatton, alive in its cradle. Then deeper in the ruins were found two or three women-servants alive, and the others dead, and "at last, on digging, they found the Lady Hatton, who was on her knees, with a wrapping-gown on, and her woman with her in the same posture, but they were both dead." And Chapple heard his lordship declare: "That soon after he was in bed he heard it thunder as at a distance, that it still came nearer and nearer, the wind growing higher, and some hail beat against the windows pretty hard; and at last he felt the bed whereon he lay move, and immediately a prodigious burst, and at the same time found himself in the open

[1] Afterwards Countess of Nottingham.

air . . . but did not apprehend that his bed had been carried out of the house, but only thought that he had fallen with it, but some very large flashes of lightning immediately following, he did, on raising himself up by the light thereof, perceive the sea on one side of him, and part of the Castle wall on the other, and therefore kept calling out for help."

A manuscript quoted by Mr. Tupper[1] adds further details to this extraordinary story. A Sergeant Cotton was blown in his bed over a high wall, and when he recovered consciousness he proceeded, naked and shivering, to the south point, where he was seen by the sentinel, who challenged him, though thinking that he was a ghost. "Nevertheless, standing upon his punctilios, [he] made the Ghost to speak, who, knowing him by his voice, settled his spirits, and so the Sergeant did bid him come and help, at which saying the centinell was much surprised, having heard nothing of the blow, for the wind carried it away from him."

Seven people were killed in this disastrous occurrence, and several were wounded. The house from which Lord Hatton had been blown was, with the exception of the doorposts, razed to the ground, and the old tower of the Castle was also completely destroyed. The people of Guernsey were horror-stricken at the sad event, and the Royal Court, deeming it an especial act of Divine vengeance, appointed the ensuing January 15 as a fast day.

From this period Castle Cornet ceased to be the resi-

---

[1] *History of Guernsey*, second edition, p. 374.

dence either of the Governors or of political prisoners. Willingly or of necessity, various interesting personages had in the preceding century inhabited it. Among them were Lucy St. John, the wife of Sir Allen Apsley and mother of Mrs. Hutchinson, who wrote the well-known memoirs of Colonel Hutchinson, her husband; Dorothy Osborne, daughter of Sir Peter, and afterwards wife of Sir William Temple; the chaplains Cartwright and Bradshaw; Burton, the Puritan divine, Prynne's colleague and fellow-sufferer, who was sent to Castle Cornet while the latter was sent to Mont Orgueil; and General Lambert. This officer so distinguished himself in the Civil War that, according to the Clarendon State Papers,[1] the first Lord Hatton wrote to Lord Chancellor Hyde suggesting that Charles II. should secure his services by offering to marry his daughter. Lord Hatton little thought that the lady he was thus recommending was destined to be his own grand-daughter-in-law. But in 1661 Lambert, disgraced and a prisoner, was exiled to Castle Cornet, bringing his two daughters, Frances and Mary, with him; and while they were immured in the grim old fortress, Lord Hatton's second son, Charles, lost his heart to Mary Lambert, and, with the connivance of three of the Islanders, clandestinely married her. Upon this his father, who had previously written of her to Clarendon as "pretty, of an extra-ordinary sweetness of disposition, and very virtuously and ingenuously disposed," wrote to the King:[2] "Your

---

[1] Quoted in Tupper's *History*, p. 353.
[2] *Notes and Queries*, Third Series, vol. iv., p. 91.

The Channel Islands

Petitioner is not ignorant that attempts have been made to suggest his misfortunes as faults in the case of his sonn's marriage with a prisoner's daughter there, and though he is confident your Majesty will not lay that as a crime to your Petitioner, yett he craves leave to say his consent could not be reasonably inferred, being to a person whose Father was attainted and who had no portion. . . . And no sooner did your Petitioner know of that match was a yeare or more after the pretended marriage, but he turned his sonn out of doores, and hath never since given him a penny."

As soon as James II. came to the throne he attempted to introduce Roman Catholicism into Guernsey by installing a Popish Governor and garrison and instituting a public celebration of the Mass. This tampering with their cherished convictions naturally excited the indignation of the Islanders, and they consequently welcomed the accession of the Protestant William III. to the throne of England, and his reign inaugurated an era of prosperity to the island.

CHAPTER VIII

THE EIGHTEENTH CENTURY

The circumstances that led to the abdication of James II. did not affect the tranquillity of Jersey; in fact, for nearly a century no important events disturbed the peace of the island. But in 1779 the smouldering enmity of France broke into flame, and the Prince of Nassau appeared with a formidable fleet off the Bay of St. Ouen and there attempted to disembark. The invaders were repulsed, however, by the 78th Regiment, assisted by the local militia; and the timely arrival of a British squadron under Sir James Wallace caused them to be nearly annihilated.

At Christmastide of the following year the French made a fresh attempt to conquer the island. On the morning of December 26, 1780, in response to a fiery signal lit the previous night between Rosel and La Coupe, two thousand French troops under the command of Philippe Charles Macquart, Baron de Rullecourt, who had accompanied the Prince of Nassau in his expedition against Jersey, embarked at Granville. They ran into a furious gale, and when de Rullecourt reached Jersey on the evening of January 5 he found his army reduced to twelve hundred men. They were piloted by Pierre Journeaux, a renegade Jerseyman, to a landing-place at the Banc de Violet, and, under cover of the darkness,

The Channel Islands

de Rullecourt landed his men and marched, totally unperceived, to the town of St. Helier.

On entering the town they killed a man called Pierre Arrivé, who was standing at his door, and in the Royal Square they killed the sentry and surprised the guard. Great was the dismay of the inhabitants when they rose the following morning to find their town full of French soldiers, without a shot having been fired or an alarm given.

The Lieutenant-Governor, who at this time was Major Moses Corbet, was asleep in his house,[1] when Captain Clement Hemery, a Jerseyman, ran to tell him of the enemy's arrival. The house was immediately surrounded and he was taken prisoner, but not before he had managed to send information by Captain Hemery to the 78th, 83rd, and 95th Regiments, who were stationed in various parts of the island.

He was then taken to the Court House, where de Rullecourt induced him to sign a capitulation, and also orders to Captain Mulcaster, commanding at Elizabeth Castle, to surrender that fortress, and to Major Peirson, commanding the remaining portion of the troops, that all his men should lay down their arms. But the former officer, saying that he " could not understand French," took not the slightest notice of these instructions; and the latter replied: "Oui, nous porterons nos armes à la Maison de Ville, mais ce sera la bayonette au bout de fusil." And immediately, reinforced by the island militia, marched towards the town with his little army,

[1] Now 25, Grosvenor Street.

The Eighteenth Century

and in a short space of time the Battle of Jersey was being fought in the Royal Square at St. Helier.

Just as the division commanded by Major Peirson entered the Square through a passage from the Rue de Derrière (now called Peirson Place) they encountered a storm of French bullets, and their gallant leader fell dead into the arms of his grenadiers. For a moment his men fell back in confusion, but when Philip Dumaresq, a young subaltern of the Jersey militia, cried out that if there was no Englishman willing to avenge his Major there was at least one Jerseyman ready to die with him, the infuriated men rushed forwards, the French were compelled to retreat, and the day was won. De Rulle-court fell, mortally wounded, and died that night in M. Lerrier's house.

The island forces lost twenty-three killed and sixty-eight wounded, the French seventy-eight killed and seventy-four wounded. Corbet, the Lieutenant-Governor, was afterwards tried by court-martial and superseded, although he was allowed by Government a pension of £250 a year.

Major Peirson was buried in the church of St. Helier, where a marble monument was erected to his memory by the people of Jersey. In the adjoining cemetery lies Baron de Rullecourt, only a few feet of earth separating the remains of the two gallant foes.

In the Court House hangs a copy of Copley's cele-brated picture representing the Battle of Jersey. Al-though it is the fashion among insular historians to stigmatise Nassau and Rullecourt as unscrupulous adventurers, we must admit that the French nation had undergone much provocation from the Islanders, who by their privateering and smuggling had destroyed the shipping and ruined the commerce of Normandy and Brittany. Bold island seamen even raided the coast itself. According to the *Gazette des Deux Ponts* of October 6, 1778, "un équipage de corsaires Jersiais descendit près de Caen et enleva des bœufs, des vaches, des moutons, tout le linge du curé et même ses deux gouvernantes qui faisaient la lessive ailleurs." While at the time of these invasions no fewer than 150 French prizes and 1,500 French seamen were in custody in Jersey.

Mindful of the bold attempt on Jersey which had thus been made by an inconspicuous Frenchman, the English authorities in later years naturally thought it necessary to increase and improve the island's defences against Napoleon. During Sir George Don's term of office as Governor (1806-14), Fort Regent was begun and nearly completed, Mont Orgueil and Fort Elizabeth were strengthened, the militia was reorganised, and the picturesque old winding lanes were straightened into military roads. The harbour also was enlarged and improved—a very necessary work, owing to the increased number of vessels England sent to protect these shores.

In 1794 Captain Philip d'Auvergne, R.N., was stationed off Jersey in the *Nonsuch*, with a flotilla of gunboats under his command for the defence of the Channel Islands, and with orders to communicate with and befriend the Royalist party on the coast of France.

The Eighteenth Century

Born in Jersey in 1754, Philip was descended from the noble French family of the Counts d'Auvergne. A cadet of this house, bearing the name of Thiebault d'Auvergne, had received a grant of land in St. Ouen's parish in 1232. In the latter part of the eighteenth century His Serene Highness Godfrey de la Tour d'Auvergne, Duc de Bouillon, was in want of a representative of his line to whom he might bequeath his title and vast wealth. About this time Lieutenant Philip d'Auvergne, being then a prisoner of war in France, was introduced to the Duke, who decided that in him he had at last found his long-sought heir. After employing experts to trace the descent of the Jersey family of d'Auvergne, the Duke in 1786 issued Letters Patent, under his own seal and signature, acknowledging Charles d'Auvergne and General d'Auvergne (father and uncle of Philip) to be descended from the ancient Counts d'Auvergne, confirming to them the armorial bearings of his family, and, with the consent of His Britannic Majesty, formally adopting Philip d'Auvergne as his son and heir.

Notwithstanding the Duke's attempt to bribe him to exchange the service of England for that of France, Philip elected to remain in the English navy, and ultimately he attained the rank of a Vice-Admiral.

In 1802, after the death of the Duke, Philip went to Paris to claim his inheritance, which had been appropriated by the French Republic. But the Consular Government had not forgotten or forgiven the services he had rendered the Royalists while serving in the

English Channel. He was immediately arrested and thrown into prison, his papers were seized, and after a few days of ill-treatment he was turned out of France.

After the restoration of the Bourbons he was, for a short time, put into nominal possession of his inheritance; but by an Act of the Congress of Vienna, upon "considerations of general policy," his claims were finally set aside in favour of Prince Charles de Rohan Guéménée, another far-away relative of the late Duke.

This final disappointment, coming after so many others, may well have made Philip feel with Gloucester—

> " As flies to wanton boys, are we to the gods;
> They kill us for their sport "—

and he retired to London, where he died in an hotel on September 18, 1816, just a year and a half after his only son had died on board ship off Colombo.

While Philip d'Auvergne was stationed in Jersey, he had shown his gratitude to his French relatives by taking under his special protection the many French refugees who fled thither from the fury of the Revolution. Between 1790 and 1793 more than four thousand Royalists, principally ecclesiastics and representatives of the French *noblesse*, sought safety in the island. There were not enough buildings to house them, and in a very short space of time the town of St. Helier doubled in size. Among these came René de Chateaubriand, the famous author of *Mémoires d'Outre-Tombe* and other works. Even as late as 1815 the Duc de Berri, who was doomed a few years later to die at the Paris Opera

PORTELET BAY, JERSEY.

by the hand of an assassin, was glad to escape to the island for a month or two.

In the middle of the nineteenth century it was the turn of the French Republicans to flee to Jersey. Pierre le Roux, Théophile Guérin, Paul Meurice, Auguste Vacquerie, Madame de Girardin, and, in 1852, most celebrated of all, Victor Hugo, were among the political exiles.

They started a newspaper among themselves called *L'Homme*, in which all kings and rulers were held up to execration. This paper in October, 1855, reproduced a scurrilous letter which had been written and published in London by a Frenchman called Félix Pyat on the subject of Queen Victoria's recent visit to Paris. The greatest excitement was caused by this lampoon, an "indignation meeting" was called, the paper was publicly burnt, and the three men principally concerned in its production were immediately sent out of the island. On this Victor Hugo wrote a strongly-worded protest, terminating with the exclamation, "Et maintenant expulsez-nous!" which he called the "Déclaration des Proscrits," and which was signed by a large number of his fellow-countrymen. Therein he complained that in a land which boasted of the liberty of its Press his compatriots had been banished, without even a trial, simply for reprinting a letter which had been published without comment or consequences in England. This protest roused deep feeling on both sides of the Channel, and it was decided by the Governor that Victor Hugo and all those who signed this document must also leave Jersey.

The Channel Islands

Some went to England, some to Spain; Victor Hugo went to Guernsey, landing at St. Peter-Port October 31, 1855.

Since Hugo's departure General Boulanger has been perhaps the most important political claimant to Jersey hospitality, which has more recently been extended to a large number of representatives of religious orders driven out of France.

During the eighteenth century Jersey society was divided into two parties, whose mutual hatred was as great as that of the Whigs and Tories in England. Their origin was as follows.[1]

In the year 1776 Charles Lemprière, Seigneur of Rosel, was Lieutenant-Bailiff of Jersey, the Bailiff at that time being his cousin, Lord Carteret, who spent so much of his time out of the island that Mr. Lemprière felt he was himself Bailiff in all but name. As we know, in those days the number of advocates was limited to six, and they were appointed by the Bailiff alone. Mr. Lemprière promised the next vacancy at the Bar to a man called Ricard; but another Jerseyman, Mr. Jean Dumaresq,[2] went off secretly to London, saw Lord Carteret, and obtained the appointment from him

[1] *Ville de St. Helier*, pp. 157-63.

[2] He had originally been engaged to Mr. Lemprière's daughter but broke it off, with the result noted above. He afterwards married Miss Mary de Mesurier, daughter of John le Mesurier, Governor of Alderney. He became Attorney-General, was named Lieutenant-Bailiff by Lord Carteret on January 7, 1802, and resigned his office in 1816. He lived at St. Peter's House, the residence of the present Bailiff of Jersey (Mr. Nicolle's MSS.).

without consulting Mr. Lemprière in the matter. This was taken by the Lieutenant-Bailiff to be a covert insult, and his anger against Dumaresq soon broke out in the Court House, where disgraceful personalities were exchanged between them. All Jersey took sides with one or other of the opponents, the partisans of Charles Lemprière being called *Charlots*, and those of Jean Dumaresq *Jeannots*, though the latter, owing to an after-dinner epigram, were soon after given the name of *Magots*.

About 1817, at the election of a jurat, the Charlots decorated their houses with branches of laurel, while the Magots used roses as their emblem, and thus the names of the factions were changed into *Les Lauriers* and *Les Roses*. The Lauriers represented the Tory or Conservative party, the Roses were Whigs or Radicals, and these two factions included the entire population of Jersey.

Time has now softened all these asperities, and only in the parish of St. Ouen do any vestiges of them remain; but their former violence may be judged from the words of Inglis,[1] an English resident, who wrote in 1834 : " It is utterly impossible for anyone unacquainted with Jersey to form any idea of the lengths to which party spirit is carried there. It not only taints the fountains of public justice, but enters into the most private relations of life. A Laurel and a Rose man are as distinct, and have as little in common between them, as if they were men, not only of different countries, but of coun-

---

[1] *The Channel Islands*, pp. 105-6.

The Channel Islands

tries hostile to each other. . . . A great mass of the country people, and tradespeople of the towns also, are of one party; and in their tenacious adherence to that party they believe that they are defending their island privileges, which they allege are constantly attacked by the party of the better educated and higher classes."

The local Press took up and fostered the quarrel, and each party had its official organ, which belaboured its opponents in the true spirit and style of the *Eatanswill Gazette*. And although the Jersey people possess many attractive qualities, yet a vehement party spirit must be reckoned among their especial attributes. Their own writer, Payne,[1] sums up their characteristics by saying that they are distinguished by "great and proverbial powers of memory, much and genuine hospitality, an innate and Hibernianesque wit, with which is curiously blended the phlegm and frugality of the cannie Scot, an incurable mania for petty political intrigue, and a native bravery that needs no other eulogy than it has already gained in the annals of the island."

[1] *Armorial*, p. 11.

GRÈVE AU LANÇON, PLEMONT, JERSEY.

CHAPTER IX

PRIVATEERING AND SMUGGLING

THE commercial history of the Islands may roughly be divided into five periods. The first of these was the fishing period, when the majority of the Islanders were seamen, and salted and dried their congers at the seigneurs' *esperqueries*. They then supplied these fish to the inhabitants of the neighbouring coasts of France and England; for in those days, when the Romish Church imposed continual fasts, fish formed the staple article of diet. The second was the knitting period, when wool was their chief import, and stockings, "guernseys," and "jerseys"—"wherein," as Dr. Heylyn says, "the inhabitants are exceeding cunning"—their chief export. This period began at the proclamation of neutrality in the fifteenth century and lasted till about the middle of the seventeenth century. The third was the privateering period, which was marked by great activity in shipbuilding and the opening up of the trade with Newfoundland. This was the time of the greatest increase in wealth, and may be said to have lasted from the middle of the seventeenth century to Waterloo. The fourth was the smuggling period, which was concurrent with the end of the third period, and practically lasted till the repeal of high duties in England rendered the business no longer profitable. The fifth is the present period of commerce and agriculture, of the exportation of granite and farm and greenhouse produce, and dates from the time when the regular service of steamboats gave quick communication with populous centres.

It is with the third and fourth periods, and particularly in their relation to Guernsey, that this chapter has to do.

There is nowadays a good deal of misapprehension as to what privateering really was. Most people regard it as simply another word for piracy; but undoubtedly in olden times, under the authorisation of proper letters of marque and subject to perfectly definite rules, it was held to be quite a justifiable and honourable occupation, and its votaries, instead of being the rollicking buccaneers of popular fancy, with pistols and cutlasses protruding from the belts fastened round their waists, with red handkerchiefs tied round their heads, and with the prospect of a rope at the yard-arm of some virtuous man-of-war or a watery grave from the end of a plank as their ultimate fate, were generally honest, hard-working, brave men, who fought for their masters and their country, and were perfectly legitimate and fully recognised belligerents. The essential characteristic of privateers was that they should be regularly commissioned by a responsible Government, although they were owned and manned by private individuals; and in the wars of past centuries, when the naval forces of great Powers were far weaker than they are now, these ships reinforced the fleet of their country and undertook duties which the king's ships were not numerous enough to perform.

Privateering and Smuggling

A letter of marque was engrossed on a large sheet of parchment, headed by an elaborate piece of scroll work, containing a portrait of the Sovereign, together with the Royal Arms and various symbolic figures. Appended was the Great Seal of the High Court of Admiralty of England. Each letter, after minutely describing the ship for which it was issued, its tonnage and armament, went on to say that " We do license and authorise (John Smith) to set forth in a warlike manner the said ship (*Arethusa*) under his own command, and therewith by force of Arms to apprehend, seize, and take the ships, vessels, and goods belonging to the King (of whatever country England was then at war with) or his subjects . . . and to bring the same to such Port as shall be most convenient, in order to have them legally adjudged in Our said High Court of Admiralty . . . after which it may be lawful (for the said John Smith) to sell and dispose of such ships, goods," etc.

The captain was ordered to keep an " exact Journal of his Proceedings," and to get all the information he could respecting the enemy's forces, and report it to the Commissioners, and all allied states were requested to give " all Aid, Assistance, and Succour in their Ports to the said captain, ship, company, and prizes, without doing or suffering to be done to him any wrong, trouble, or hindrance, We offering to do the like when We shall be thereunto desired. . . . In witness whereof We have caused this great Seal of Our said Court to be hereunto affixed."

The captain of the vessel also entered into formal

agreements with his crew. For example, the man who first saw a sail, or first boarded an enemy's ship, was to receive four guineas. After the captured ship and her cargo were sold, the money was divided into stipulated shares. One-fifth went to the King, who in 1698 had an accredited agent in Guernsey, Mr. Robert Lee, to collect these dues;[1] of the remainder, two-thirds went to the owner of the vessel and one-third to the captain, officers, and crew according to seniority.

Sir George Carteret's "pataches" had shown the Islanders how profitable a trade privateering could be, and they were not slow in taking example by his enterprise.

As early as 1667 we find Colonel Atkins, Lieutenant-Governor of Guernsey, thus writing to Mr. Amias Andros:[2] "I cannot omitt to relate how bravelie the men of St. Martyn's have behaved themselves at sea. They have brought in a prize of sixty tun, a flie boate belonging to Amsterdam, laden with wine, ptum,[3] figs, and rosin. . . . They likewise encountered with another at sea, of nyne or ten guns, with their two guns, of which they were fayne to borrow one of mee; but received so much damage . . . and having ffive of their twenty-ffive men hurt, they were forced to leave her; but manfully after this tooke the same. . . . I have given you this relation that you may see your countrymen will fight."

---

[1] This appears from some Actes des États for 1698.

[2] Tupper's *History*, p. 368.

[3] *Ptum* for *petun*, an old French and American word derived from *petunam*, for tobacco. It is still used in Sark and Jersey.

Privateering and Smuggling

The Treaty of Neutrality had by this time become virtually a dead letter, and it was finally abrogated in 1689 by William III. on the ground that it formed an easy means for James II. to communicate with his partisans in England. No opposition was raised by the Islanders to this measure, as they had discovered that war was far more profitable to them than peace.

One of the most famous privateer captains known in local history was Captain John Tupper of the *Monmouth Galley*, a great-great-grandson of one Henry Tupper who fled from Hesse-Cassel in consequence of an edict issued by Charles V. against the Lutherans. In the Public Record Office[1] is an order issued to the Treasurer of the Navy and dated October 22, 1694, "for the sum of Fifty Pounds . . . to provide a Medall and chaine of that value, for Captain John Tupper, Commander of a privateer called the *Monmouth Galley* of Guernsey, as a reward to him for his good services in destroying some French privateers."

The following quotations from contemporary letters[2] preserved in the Admiralty Records give some slight idea of the work performed by the privateersmen of that epoch. The first is from this very Captain Tupper, then in command of the privateer the *Swallow*, dated Guernsey, August 26, 1692. "This is duly to advise you that after many attempts at sea I returned cruiseing out of this port on the 16th inst., the 17th and 18th

[1] Lords' Letter-Book, 1694-5, vol. vii.
[2] Printed in full in *The Clan*, edited by Colonel John Glas Sandeman, vol. ii. (1897), pp. 147-8.

The Channel Islands

following, being under Cape Frenely nere St. Maloes we mett with Eight great ships coming from thence. Three of them bore upon us, but perceiving they could have noe advantage they immediately joyned their squadron and bore to the West North West, soe being divided wee kept our course upon the coast, soe nere that we could easily see Thirteen very great ships wth many other small ones in St. Malloes Roade. The 19th following I took a small fishing boate in the Road of Granville, which after examinacon of the men I sett at liberty, considerin^g their great necessity and weakness, they informed me that the French Soldiers wch were upon the coast were gone towards Rochel and nothing else worth your advice. The Sunday following I mett with three French Copers, giving chase to Captain Major of Jersey and Captn Stevens[1] of this Island, Privat^r, being cleare of them, the same day about four of the clock in the afternoon we mett with an English vessel coming from Boston in New England, bound for London, wch had been taken by the French nere Cape Clere upon the coast of Ireland the Thursday before, wch s^d vessel Captn Stevens and I after a short dispute boarded her and brought her the day fol-

---

[1] Captain Stevens was a member of the old Guernsey family of Estienne, and this is a curious instance of how local names became anglicised. His son, in some old letters which are still extant, was called indifferently *Stevens* or *Estienne*, according to the language the letter was written in. Many other Channel Islands names suffered similar changes when their owners were brought into contact with English people. Thus, among others, the names of le Roy la Cloche, le Moyne, Pageot, and Henry, became *King*, *Bell*, *Monk*, *Paget*, and *Harris*.

lowing into this Port. She is about ninety tons, her first voyage, laden with Sugar, Molasses, Fish, Oyle, Beav^r Skins, and Logg and Brazell wood, Cotton, Wool, supposed to be worth £3,000."

Tupper's coadjutor, Captain Stevens, commander of the *Guernsey*, in a letter dated Guernsey, August 24, 1692, gives further particulars of this " short dispute " : " The next day being Sunday . . . I spied four ships going along shore and I made after them, so comeing almost within gunshot of them, Two of them being French Privateers, one of Eight guns and the other of Ten, they tacked after me so I was forced to run from them, and stood towards Captn John Major, a Privateer of Jersey, but he seeing that they gave me chase he made all the Saile he could from me, but some tyme after I spyd a saile at sea, whom I made to be Captn Tupper of Guernsey. I made the signall to him and he answered me, then being certain it was him and that I knew he would stand by me I brought too to stay for the French Privateers, but they seeing there was two of us that would stand one by the other they made the best of their way for St. Mallo's. . . . Now in the afternoon, Captn Major being about a league and a half ahead of me, I spied another ship that was ahead of him, then immediately Captn Tupper and I gave the said ship chase, and Captn Major, supposing it was another French Privateer, got his tacks on board and stood to the Northward, and Captn Tupper and I being the best sailers I came within gunshott, they immediately put out English colours with the cross downwards, then I fired at him and he put down his colours and fired at me, soe continuing for a matter of an hour, then by that time I came along his side and fired a broadside and a volley of small shott and made him strike, then Captn Tupper came up with us, and being consorts, we put some of his and my men aboard and brought her into this place."

From a list compiled by the late Dr. Hoskins,[1] it appears that at the beginning of Queen Anne's reign, during the War of the Succession, the largest Guernsey owner of privateers was Pierre Henry, who had six; that one of his captains, Pierre le Roux, was taken prisoner in an engagement; and that £425 had to be paid for his ransom. Other owners were Elisha Dobrée of the *Nottingham*, John Tupper of the *Guernsey Galley*, and Peter Carey of the *Guernsey Frigate*.

During the Seven Years' War, which began in 1755, the number of Guernsey privateers greatly increased. One of the finest was the *Bellona*, and her fate is related in a quaint inscription on a monument in the parish church of St. Peter-Port: "Sacred to the memory of Captn Nicholas le Messurier, Commander of the Private Ship of War the *Bellona* of twenty guns, belonging to this Island, Who being on a Cruise, in the night of the twelfth of February, 1759, fell in with a large French India ship, and in the morning by dawn of day gallantly attack'd, and engaged her, but about an hour after was unfortunately slain. The Privateer being greatly shatter'd in her Masts and Rigging, having several shot betwixt wind and water, and many Men kill'd and

[1] MSS. at Candie Library.

GUERNSEY FROM FORT GEORGE.

wounded, was obliged to sheer off, after having greatly shatter'd the Enemy. He was a Native of this Island. Born the 16th of May, in the year 1731, and always behav'd like a brave and diligent Officer; to whose memory the Owners of the Privateer have erected this Monument out of Gratitude for his good Services."

The *Resolution*, belonging to two brothers of the name of le Mesurier, with a crew of one hundred men and carrying twenty guns, in 1779 captured three prizes worth £134,589. In the same year, John Tupper, junior, with his cutter, the *Hector*, and two brigs, the *Lord Amherst* and the *Triumph*, each manned with sixteen guns and carrying crews of sixty-five men, captured eight prizes, to the value of £59,374. And in 1782, John le Mesurier, Governor of Alderney, owned eight privateers carrying from four to twenty guns, which brought him prize money to the value of £212,381.

Naturally, when such golden results might be expected, the fitting out of privateers went on rapidly. It was a sort of gambling speculation and one of a most exciting nature, for the vessel might be captured within twenty-four hours of leaving port, or she might send home a dozen valuable prizes in a cruise of as many days. In the year 1800, it was calculated that the money brought into the island by the captures of French and American vessels amounted to nearly a million pounds sterling. In that one year, thirty-five more ships, carrying 250 guns and 1,716 men, were fitted out in the island, principally by members of the Priaulx, Dobrée, le Mesurier, and le Cocq families, and the value of their captures amounted to very nearly another million pounds. The Governor of Cherbourg wrote to Paris that the two islands, Jersey and Guernsey, were the despair of France at the breaking out of each war, that the habit of encountering the dangers of the sea rendered the natives very brave, and that though they were good neighbours during peace, and closely united by the contraband trade which enriched them as well as the inhabitants of the neighbouring coasts of Brittany and Normandy, they became formidable enemies when war was declared. So formidable, indeed, was their enmity, and so valuable the assistance which they rendered to England, that Burke declared in Parliament that they were almost entitled to be called " one of the naval powers of the world." It was not until the Declaration of Paris, April 16, 1856, that the countries of Europe formally agreed that " Privateering is and remains abolished."

At the same time that the island of Guernsey was reaping so rich a harvest through its privateers, many of its inhabitants were also engaged in the less laudable but hardly less lucrative occupation of smuggling. The Custom House dues in those days were enormous. In 1660, no fewer than 1,630 articles were taxed in England, and as late as 1797 some twelve hundred articles were taxed, including almost every necessary of life. The inhabitants of the Channel Islands, like all the population of the South Coast of England, had come to regard the defrauding of the revenue as a perfectly justifiable method of asserting their natural right to buy their goods in the cheapest market. They considered

Privateering and Smuggling

the enforcement of the laws against smuggling to be an encroachment on their ancient rights and privileges, and claimed total exemption from the Excise laws and Customs regulations of Great Britain. As early as 1709 the States of Guernsey obtained an Order in Council revoking the permission which had been granted to the Custom House authorities to establish themselves in the island; and in 1717, 1720, and 1722 they refused to allow any kind of *Douane* to be instituted. In 1767, however, the English Government insisted on establishing a Custom House, and sent over a Mr. James Major in an armed cruiser to see that their orders were duly carried out. But this action aroused a chorus of protest, led by Mr. William le Marchant, one of the jurats, and afterwards Bailiff of the island, who issued a pamphlet on the subject, called " The Rights and Immunities of the Island of Guernsey "; and virtually matters went on pretty much as before.

Mr. Shore[1] tells us that " the chief entrepôt for the smuggling trade with England during the greater part of last century and the early years of the present one was at the Channel Islands; and of this very lucrative business Guernsey monopolised by far the larger share. . . . Owing to certain climatic conditions this island had become a favourite place with the merchants of Bordeaux and elsewhere for the storage of wines, which here developed certain qualities of excellence unattainable elsewhere, and this led to the construction of the enor-

[1] *Smuggling Days and Smuggling Ways,* by Lieutenant the Hon. H. N. Shore, R.N. (1892), pp. 84 and 89.

mous cellars which were subsequently utilised for the storage of spirits." So great was this deposit of spirits, that one family was reported to have amassed a fortune of £300,000 by the manufacture of casks alone. As Mr. Gallienne says in his "Reminiscences,"[1] "our stores along the quay, in Truchot Street, in Bordage and Park Street, in fact all over the town, were overflowing with casks of wine and of spirits; the shipping from Spain and France filled our little harbour. From England came tight sea boats with ample crews of hardy men who called themselves 'free-traders.' Guernsey people made no enquiries; they sold honest merchandise at honest prices: what came of it was none of their business. And so coopering went on briskly; small handy casks that one man could carry were in great request, and there was no return of empties."

In the last quarter of 1800, the Bailiff and two of the jurats owned to having exported 3,325 pipes and 983 hogsheads of brandy and wine, and Mr. Tupper tells us[2] that it was no uncommon occurrence for a merchant of Rotterdam to receive an order from Guernsey for one thousand pipes of gin.

In 1807 the Islands were definitely included in the English Smuggling Act, and a large share of the old trade was then transferred to Roscoff, a small village on the coast of Brittany within a few hours' sail of Guernsey. The majority of the Islanders, seeing that further remonstrance was useless, established under the auspices of Messrs. Daniel de Lisle Brock, Bailiff, Bonamy

---

[1] Guernsey *Star*, January 24, 1901. [2] *History*, 502 n.

Privateering and Smuggling

Dobrée, Thomas Priaulx, and other leading men, in December 1808, a Chamber of Commerce, the condition of membership being a promise to discontinue all illicit traffic. Yet a certain percentage of the lower classes of the people still continued to smuggle, though far more clandestinely than before. Tobacco, in many cases, took the place of spirits, and many secret hiding-places and *caches* are still to be found under the cliffs and in the old farmhouses in the vicinity of the sea-coast; and undoubtedly many of the still current legends of ghostly processions and funeral cortèges were started by these smugglers in order to distract attention from their gangs as they passed at midnight in single file along narrow lanes, with their kegs upon their shoulders, to some appointed rendezvous.

Victor Hugo[1] has well expressed the feelings with which nowadays we look back upon "ces vieux marins furtifs et farouches, naviguant jadis, en des chaloupes sans boussole, sur les vagues noires lividement éclairées, de loin en loin, de promontoire en promontoire, par ces antiques brasiers à frissons de flammes, que tourmentaient dans des cages de fer les immenses vents des profondeurs."

Thanks to privateering and smuggling, and to such trades as shipbuilding and coopering, which they so largely developed, some families found themselves raised in the course of a few years from the lowest depths of poverty to absolute wealth; and this naturally led to great disorganisation of the social life of the community.

[1] *L'Archipel de la Manche*, p. 88.

The Channel Islands

In January 1780 twenty members of the old island aristocracy had bought a site in the market-place for the erection of "Assembly Rooms," where they and their friends could hold balls and parties, which had before been held in rooms in the Pollet. These Assembly Rooms cost £2,300, and constituted a local " Almack's." A stringent code of rules was issued, some of which sound rather odd to modern ideas. For instance: (1) "The Assemblies to open at seven, and to close at half-past eleven." (4) "Ladies sitting down during a dance, to stand at the bottom during the remainder of the evening." (7) "No native inhabitant, whose parents have not previously subscribed, to be admitted, unless proposed by the Master of the Ceremonies, and approved of by two-thirds of the ladies and gentlemen subscribers present. None but native inhabitants entitled to vote." (8) "It is to be observed by every native inhabitant, proposed to become a subscriber to these rooms, that his name shall be publicly mentioned to the Master of Ceremonies, and by him to the native subscribers, a fortnight, at least, before the meeting."

It was these two latter rules that created the social conflicts which agitated Guernsey in the early decades of the nineteenth century. The original subscribers, with their families, and with the naval and military officers quartered in the island, numbered about sixty people; and they alone were entitled to the enjoyment of the rooms. But in the course of the next thirty years many young men and girls grew up, whose fathers, though *nouveaux riches* and not in a position to have been

146

original subscribers to the rooms, had yet amassed sufficient wealth to give their children good educations and
keep them at home, and it was in this way that the difficulty began.   These young people, of course, wished to
enjoy themselves at the "Assemblies," but they had to
be elected first, and when, time after time, admittance
was denied them, naturally a very bitter feeling was
engendered.   Excluded from the balls of "the Sixties,"
the name of "the Forties" was applied to them, and
thus arose the factions of two generations ago, whose
mutual hatred was as great as that of the *Roses* and
Laurels of Jersey, and none the less that the feelings
which inspired it were entirely social, and not, as in the
sister island, in any sense political.

Nowadays these distinctions are virtually ignored, and
the whirligig of time has brought in his revenges.   For
the old Assembly Rooms, whose portals were once so
jealously guarded, were sold some years ago to Messrs.
Guille and Allès for the library with which they muni-
ficently endowed their native island, and are therefore
open to every subscriber, though probably but few of
those who sit there reading magazines or newspapers
think of the

> " dear dead cotillons,
> Danced out in tumult long before you came."

PETIT PORTELET BAY. JERSEY.

CHAPTER X

THE ISLAND OF JERSEY

ALMOST every Islander knows from sad experience how dreary and tempestuous the English Channel can be, and has approached his journey's end—with feelings of devout thankfulness that the voyage is so nearly over—to find the coasts shrouded in mist and foam, and the cold, grey waves heaving under him even in harbour. But fortunately it is not always thus, and nothing can be more delightful on a brilliant summer morning than to steam along the coast of Jersey and to watch each well-known point rise into view.

After Grosnez is passed come the cruel jagged peaks of the Corbière, culminating in the straight, white spire of the lighthouse. Such great mysterious rocks lie around each of the islands that they give the impression of being the self-appointed guardians of their native shores; some of them resemble strange sea-monsters just come up to breathe, others are like gaunt priests, weird women, or giant warriors with their feet wrapped in foam. How many would-be invaders, both friends and foes, have they lain in wait for, wrestled with, and overcome in the days gone by?

Behind them follow a succession of cool green bays, Portelet, St. Brelade, and the white sweep of sand which

The Channel Islands

forms St. Aubin's, until grey Elizabeth Castle looms on the horizon and the boat steams between the pier heads into the harbour of St. Helier. The first impression of both harbour and town is disappointing. The former is flat and colourless, and the latter, though clean and prosperous and boasting of excellent shops, has been so modernised and rebuilt that almost all its individuality has been destroyed, and it is now very much like Ryde, Southsea, or any modern English watering-place.

The most interesting spot to be found within it is the Royal Square—the old market-place. Here the Battle of Jersey was fought and gallant Peirson fell, here is the modern Court House on the site of the old Cohue Royale—where almost every important event in Jersey history has either been discussed or taken place —and here is the splendid library founded by Falle, one of Jersey's earliest historians. In the centre of the square is a gilt statue, erected in 1751 on the site of the old market cross, and said to represent George II.

At the bottom of the square, towards the sea, lies the parish church of St. Helier, an old brown Norman building with a low square tower. It contains many interesting monuments, notably that to the memory of Major Peirson.

In a neighbouring street stands the Museum of the Société Jersiaise, where relics of the past and information relating to the history and literature of the island are collected and preserved. The most valuable treasure it contains is the magnificent gold torque, which was found most charming old church imaginable, with grey granite walls, arched doorways, a stone roof, and a belfry composed of an isolated turret. Beside it, and enclosed in the same churchyard—for the dead are here "entomb'd upon the very hem o' the sea"—stands the Chapelle ès Pêcheurs, a plain oblong building, whose walls display a few remnants of old frescoes, with a vaulted stone roof, with loopholes for windows, and surmounted by a tiny stone cross, so old and roughly hewn that it bends forward, looking like a little grey monk with downcast head and folded arms.

Tradition says that this is the oldest Christian edifice in the Islands, and was built by St. Marcouf for the fishermen, as its name denotes. Just beyond it again is the jetty built by those very Norman fisherfolk who came to the chapel to pray, and then come tall granite rocks and the sea; and here in this little corner, consecrated by more than a thousand years of simple faith, all seems unchanged and unspoilt, and as it may have appeared when the Gospel of Christ was first preached in the Islands.

East of St. Helier, beyond the orchards of Samarès and the little fishing village of Pontac, lie long stretches of furze, sand, and outlying rocks ending in the curve of Gorey Bay, which is dominated by the castle of Mont Orgueil. Nothing in the other islands can attempt to rival Mont Orgueil in beauty or in interest. Like Stirling and like some of the Rhineland castles, it appears to have grown out of the solid rock, "Fragments of stone, reared by creatures of clay." From its summit on clear days the triple towers of the cathedral of Coutances are plainly visible. The old keep of the castle and one turret are fairly intact, but the rest is now only a mass of magnificent fragments, arches and ruins of arches, stone stairways—which still seem to echo with the clank of mailed feet—terminating abruptly in some isolated doorway, a lone belfry, or a grassy plateau, and over everything a drapery of lichens and ivy, while between the crevices and revelling upon the crumbling ramparts (like children playing among graves) are brilliant bushes of golden wallflowers.

The northern side of the island presents characteristics very different from those of the south. Its shores, instead of gently sloping from the sea, rise up in rugged cliffs of desolate grandeur broken up into beautiful bays and inlets—Verclut, Anne Port, St. Catherine's, and many others. Bouley Bay is perhaps the finest of all, with its outline of gigantic rocks that stretch from the Tour de Rosel to Belle Hougue. This bit of Jersey, as Hugo says, recalls the precipitous coasts of Brittany, while the south, with its orchards and luxuriant vegetation, is like "la belle Normandie."

The general impression given by the whole island, with its balmy climate and semi-tropical vegetation, is of unbounded fertility and prosperity, and this impression is intensified by the fine old parish churches as well as the charming manor-houses embowered in trees, with which the country is interspersed. The houses are like those which Aubrey depicted—"a high strong wall, a gatehouse, a great hall and parlours, and within the little green court the barne, for they think not the noise of the threshold ill musique." The manor-house of St. Ouen for age, grandeur, and beauty ranks before all others, but Rosel, La Hague, Noirmont, the two Vinchelez, Longueville, and many others, "built for pleasure and for state," testify to the refinement and taste of Jersey's ancient lords of the soil.

It is not surprising that an island possessed of such heroic traditions and such beautiful scenery should have given birth to warriors like the de Carterets, the Lemprières, the Dumaresqs, the Durells, and le Hardys, to say nothing of the many who distinguished themselves in South Africa and in the Great War, where 800 Jerseymen were killed or died and 8,000 served both on sea and land; or to artists like Monamy, le Capelain, Philip Jean, Mr. Ouless, R.A., Mr. St. Helier Lander, the famous portrait painter, Mr. Edmund Blampied, Mr. Le Maistre, and, greatest of them all, Sir John Millais. In the paths of literature, moreover, Jersey-men have been well known since the days of Wace. Among the local historians and antiquaries—besides many who are happily still alive—are found the names of Poingdestre, Falle, le Geyt, le Quesne, Durell, etc.; and such well-known authors as Morant, the historian of Essex, and Lemprière, of the *Classical Dictionary*, Dr. Brevint, Dr. Valpy, and Bishop Jeune, and such legal luminaries as the late Lord St. Helier, Mr. Justice Bailhache, and others, too numerous to mention, claim Jersey as their native land.

L'ETAC, JERSEY.

CHAPTER XI

THE ISLAND OF GUERNSEY

ONE of the most beautiful sights in the whole Channel Archipelago is the view as you enter Guernsey Harbour on a brilliant summer morning. To the north stands on a slight eminence the old Vale Castle, guardian of the busy little port of St. Sampson. Sombre Castle Cornet, which seems to bar all approach, lies opposite the town, and in the quiet pool is gathered every variety of shipping—white yachts, black barges, cinnamon-sailed fishing-boats, silhouetted against the tall irregular houses which line the quay. The town of St. Peter-Port is built on the slope of a hill, with tier upon tier of tall red-roofed houses clustering down to the water's edge. It is protected on the southern side by the green height on which Fort George is situated, and behind that again the rocky promontory of Jerbourg, beyond which, when veiled in the morning mists that make sea and sky seem one, the horizon melts away into a golden haze woven of cloud and sunshine.

The town retains a certain amount of its former picturesqueness, though many of its old landmarks have been swept away. Built on the side of a hill, it is traversed by a curious succession of long stairways, with cross lanes meeting at the "carrefours," leading up to other and still quainter and narrower steps, and to dark arched alleys. The whole town has a foreign appearance—"Caudebec sur les épaules de Honfleur," as Vacquerie describes it.

Its most interesting building is the parish church—a Norman cruciform edifice, which has been called the cathedral of the Channel Islands. The popular notion is that it was consecrated in 1312, but this is derived from a spurious document called the "Dédicace des Églises," which, though accepted by Guernsey's early historians, has been proved by modern savants to be a forgery from beginning to end. The church was in existence in 1048, but no vestige of the original building now remains. It is supposed that the oldest part of the present structure dates from the reign of King John, and it was added to in the fourteenth and fifteenth centuries, probably after being partially demolished by foreign invaders. It contains among its ecclesiastical plate an almost unique altar cruet, dating from the early part of the sixteenth century. St. Peter-Port is fortunate in possessing two splendid libraries—the Guille-Allès, founded and endowed by two patriotic Guernseymen, Messrs. Thomas Guille and Frederick Allès; and Candie, formed and bequeathed to his native island by that eminent bibliophile, Mr. Osmond de Beauvoir Priaulx. It can also boast of two most excellent museums—the Guille-Allès and the Lukis, the latter containing a wonderful collection of neolithic implements, pottery, etc., found in the local dolmens.

The scenery of the interior of the island has been quite

The Island of Guernsey

ruined by the miles of greenhouses and the ugly little workmen's cottages and bungalows which have been built all over it. The old flower-clad hedges have been destroyed, and almost every tree cut down. Indeed, except for the grounds of a few gentlemen's houses—such as Saumarez Park, Sausmarez Manor, the Haye du Puits, St. George, and Le Vallon—Guernsey is practically treeless, and only here and there does some deep fern-clad well, or a forgotten lane, "with ivy canopied, and interwove with flaunting honeysuckle," recall the former beauty of this once lovely island. Even the shores are now being spoilt, and all the southern coast from Jerbourg Point to Pleinmont, with its magnificent rocky headlands and its storm-stained ravines surmounted by flower-clad cliffs, and intersected with small green valleys undulating "as if God's finger touched but did not press," is now being ruined by architectural atrocities. Moulin Huet Bay is perhaps the most lovely spot in the Islands, partially hemmed in as it is with a chain of wonderful rocks, one of which has been christened "Andrelot" by the country people. To them this strange rock-figure personifies the guardian spirit of the bay, and "le petit bonhomme" still has every boat's ensign dipped in his honour and a small oblation flung to him "for luck" by the fishermen of St. Martin's parish as they sail past.

Like the other islands, Guernsey is full of interesting relics of the past, and among its people are still to be found legends of fairies and goblins and a firm belief in the power of witchcraft. The old parish churches, in spite of having been greatly mutilated in various "restorations," are very picturesque, particularly that of St. Pierre-du-Bois, which is built on so great an incline that one has to walk up a visible ascent in approaching the east end. It is in this corner of the island, from St. Pierre-du-Bois to Hommet, that most of the old-world charm of Guernsey still lingers, and it is there that the people remain most primitive. Even for the unbeliever in magic and witchcraft, what Hugo calls "le mystère des heures noires" clings to the wild western coasts of Rocquaine and Vazon, haunted as they are to every credulous countryman by the fairies of the Creux des Fées and the witches of the Catioroc, where in former years his ancestors had whispered of Saturn and his "Varous" in their subterranean caverns; while to the true Guernseyman the first whiff of the "Vraic" piled up along the shore curls speechlessly around the roots of his being, sending up a wave of feeling as inexpressible as "the joy that is more ancient than the hills."

The northern part of Guernsey, which is flat and sandy, was probably the portion first inhabited. The desolate moorland of L'Ancresse Common, now the resort of golfers, contains the finest dolmens in the island; and the ruins of two old fortresses, Vale Castle and Ivy Castle, are situated in this neighbourhood.

On the north-eastern coast the ugly, prosperous little town of St. Sampson, lying in the middle of stone quarries and greenhouses, can boast of a picturesque old church, to which belongs a most beautiful embossed chalice, which dates from about 1525. Over the read-

ST. PETER-PORT FROM THE WHITE ROCK, GUERNSEY.

in their attempt to wrest Angers from the Catholics, and they were forced to remain in exile until one day they beheld the arrival of two ships fitted out with all they required.

These Huguenots were succeeded by those who fled from the effects of the Revocation of the Edict of Nantes, of whom many, like the la Serres, de la Condamines, Durands, Métiviers, etc., married and settled in the island. Many French aristocrats also arrived during the Revolution, and in 1815 came Marshal Grouchy, masquerading as a Lyons merchant, under the name of Gautier. But Guernsey's most illustrious exile has been Victor Hugo. After his expulsion from Jersey in 1855 he arrived at St. Peter-Port and purchased Hauteville House, and "this eyrie was the homeless eagle's nest" until 1870. In 1878 he revisited it for a few months, and it still belongs to his descendants, and is the Mecca of many French pilgrims. Here were written much of his poetry and three of his best-known novels, *Les Misérables*, *L'Homme qui Rit*, and *Les Travailleurs de la Mer*. The last-named book was dedicated " au rocher d'hospitalité et de liberté, à ce coin de vieille terre Normande où vit le noble petit peuple de la mer à l'île de Guernesey, sévère et douce, mon asile actuel, mon tombeau probable." It purports to be " le poème en prose de l'archipel anglo-normand ";[1] but in spite of its author's genius, its "local colour" is entirely incorrect, and Lethierry, Clubin, Déruchette, and Gilliatt are

[1] *La Maison de Victor Hugo*, by Gustave Larroumen (Paris, 1895), p. 19.

utterly impossible representatives of Channel Islanders
of the early nineteenth century. The language which is
put into their mouths is also quite unlike Guernsey
French;[1] and the folklore, with which the book is
elaborately full, bears no resemblance to any of the
superstitions and beliefs that Guernseymen have ever
held.

The island has long been noted for the " Guernsey
lily " (*Amaryllis sarniensis*), of which the origin is not
definitely known. The tradition most generally received, and quoted by Dr. Morison,[2] is that a Dutch
vessel from Japan which had some bulbs on board was
shipwrecked off the island, "and the bulbs being washed
on shore took root in the sand, attracting notice as soon
as they bloomed by their wonderful beauty." Lord
Hatton was then Governor of that island for King
Charles II. His second son "was by good luck a
curious person and a great lover of flowers, and therefore he not only took care to transplant and cultivate
this flower himself, but sent roots of it to a great many
botanists and florists in England." This second son was
the Charles Hatton we have already met with as having
incurred his father's displeasure by clandestinely marrying Mary Lambert. He evidently inherited his love of
flowers from his father, for in the Hatton MSS. in the
British Museum[3] is a letter to Lord Hatton written in

---

[1] Thus they are made to speak of a haunted house as a *maison
visionnée*, instead of a *maison hantée*.

[2] *Plantarum Historica Oxoniensis*, Oxford, 1680.

[3] Add. MSS. 29555, fol. 221.

LADIES' BATHING-PLACE, ST. PETER-PORT, GUERNSEY.

The Island of Guernsey

and, at a conservative estimate, another 400 men were enlisted in the Royal Navy beyond the 500 who were already serving in 1914. Beyond this she also raised and maintained her own regiment, the Royal Guernsey Light Infantry, of 1,800 men, whose prowess at Haze-brouck and Cambrai earned especial mention in Lord Haig's despatches. The sad record remains of the 994 casualties and 255 prisoners of war, now represented by the 1,859 maimed, widows, and dependants from Guernsey, Alderney, and Sark, who are, in 1923, still receiving pensions in the Bailiwick. Thus the total amount of the Bailiwick's fighting men, enlisted between 1914-18, amounted to 5,700, exclusive of 530 Frenchmen returned to their native country to fight for France. The much greater proportion of Frenchmen residing in Jersey is shown by the fact that, of Jersey's 6,000 enlistments, no less than 2,300 were Frenchmen who necessarily returned to France. These figures should be looked at in the light that, by their Charters, the Islanders were exempt from all foreign service, and it was of their own free will that they temporarily abrogated their privileges.

In the domains of literature, science, and art, it is only possible here to mention Peter Paul Dobrée, Professor of Greek at Cambridge, and editor of Porson's posthumous *Aristophanica;* Dr. MacCulloch, the geologist; Doctors Lukis and Hoskins and Sir Edgar MacCulloch, archæologists and antiquaries, the last-named also the foremost authority on local folklore; Ferdinand Brock Tupper, Guernsey's historian and biographer *par ex-*

cellence; Sir Peter le Page Renouf, the eminent Egypto-logist; Paul Naftel and Peter Le Lievre, the water-colour painters; and, finally, George Métivier, poet and philo-logist, author of the *Dictionnaire Franco-Normand*, whose feelings for his native island are expressed in the following lines in the Guernsey dialect he loved so well :

> " Pour tout chunna[1] l'île est riche et belle,
> Ghernerhuia[2] mérite un p'tit luron;[3]
> A ta santaï ! a' n'a pas sa pareille,
> Où barque fliotte à vèle[4] ou aviron."

Much of the land and wealth of both Jersey and Guernsey have now passed into alien hands, and the old buildings, customs, and institutions are being treated with the Philistinism of the modern Radical, who is now a dominant factor in insular politics. Such a man even disdains the old language, although in it is centred his national literature, laws, and history.

Professor Fleure has pointed out, while referring to the small size of Guernsey : " Here might well be unification if anywhere; but yet one could map the distribution of family names, of sub-dialects of the old Norman-French *patois*, even of physical types of the population." [5]

Yet in spite of all endeavours there still lingers a certain individuality about the thoroughbred Channel Islander; to the world in general he asserts himself an

---

[1] Cela.   [2] An old form of the name Guernsey.
[3] Bagatelle, sornette.
[4] Voile.   [5] *Geographical Factors*, p. 7.

CHAPTER XII

"*THE KEY OF THE CHANNEL*"

THE island of Alderney has always been treated as the "ugly sister" of the Channel Island group; her history has been neglected and her beauty ignored, although latterly her strategic importance has been realised, and since the days when Bonaparte called her "le bouclier d'Angleterre," she has been generally acknowledged to be the key of the Channel.

The island may be physically divided into two distinct halves, the north and east consisting of low sandy commons, the south and west of huge granite cliffs, fertile uplands, and green valleys. It was in the former division that most of the Alderney dolmens and the menhir called La Pierre du Vilain[1] were situated and most of the Celtic and Roman remains and coins have been dug up. One of the most curious of these discoveries is mentioned by Holinshed. "There is," he writes, "the Isle of Alderney, a very pretty Plot, about

[1] In an ordonnance of 1609 respecting the King's newly formed rabbit warren, of which this stone formed one of the boundaries, it is thus described: "Une certaine montjoye ou monceau de pierres, servant de marque au bateaux pour la pêcherie de la mer, communement appelée le vilain, situé en une petite plaine et vallée dite Lie à Raie, qui git entre le mont appelée la Touraille et la montagne du Havre ès Corblets."

seuen miles in compasse, wherein a Priest not long since did find a coffin of stone, in which lay ye body of and [*sic*] huge Gyaunt, whose four teeth were so bigge as a man's fist, as Lelande doth report." Dr. Lukis,[1] commenting on the above extract, says that the measurement of the aforesaid cist was only seven feet four inches in length, and explains the presence of this enormous tooth by the conjecture that it may have been a fossilised fragment of some extinct animal, which had been laid in the cist with the other valuables possessed by the deceased.

One of the earliest authentic notices of Alderney is a charter[2] granted some twenty years before the Conquest of England by William, Count of the Normans, to the abbey of Mont. St. Michel; whereby he gives his islands of Sark and Alderney in exchange for the other half of Guernsey which his father Count Robert had given them for the salvation of his soul, and which he (William) had restored to Ranulph, son of Anschetil. A few years after this, however, Alderney was wrested from the monks of Mont St. Michel in spite of their remonstrances and given by William the Conqueror to Geoffrey de Mowbray, the warlike Bishop of Coutances.

Dupont[3] quotes a thirteenth-century document called the *Status Insulæ de Aurineo*, which describes the con-

---

[1] "Antiquities of Alderney," *Journal of the British Archæological Association*, April, 1847.

[2] *Calendar of Documents preserved in France*, edited by J. H. Round, p. 251.

[3] Vol. ii., pp. 103-12; and *Cartulaire de Jersey, Guernesey, etc*, 5[e] Fascicule, p. 396.

MOULIN HUET, GUERNSEY.

dition of the island about the year 1240. It was then divided equally between the King of England and the Bishop of Coutances, each claiming equal rights of jurisdiction and of *camparts*—that is, the eleventh sheaf of cereals and vegetables. Both King and Bishop had a Court presided over by a prévôt, who received the seigneurial revenues and taxes, and administered justice with the assistance of six jurats sitting alternately in either Court.[1]

The island was divided into seven *fouages*, or homesteads, and each tenant owning more than six sheep "à deux dents " had to keep and nourish one for the benefit of his seigneur. The King and the Bishop shared between them the general wreck of the sea, the King, however, reserving for himself, "par l'ancienne dignité de la duché," all gold, silk in the piece, and bales or mantles of scarlet cloth—if whole and unspotted—which might be cast up on the seashore.

Behind the town of St. Anne lies a district of arable land called the Blayes. The narrow strips of ground into which it is still divided are the outcome of the old seigneurial *droit de blairie*—a tithe claimed by each seigneur from the farmers whose cattle roamed at will through this land during the period between harvest and

---

[1] In the Assize Roll of 1309, according to the publication of the Société Jersiaise, the names of these prévôts and five of the jurats are given: William Jacob and William le Petyt, prévôts; and Peter Peset, Peter de Pleyn, James Nicole, William May, and William le Waleys, jurats. Some of these names survive in Alderney to this day. A "jury of twelve " is also mentioned by name, evidently corresponding to the parochial *douzaine*.

seed-time, but were excluded from it for the rest of the year. This custom lasted well into the nineteenth century. The letters F. and V. cut on the old weather-beaten headstones placed at certain corners of these strips are supposed to denote whether the lands were *terres franches*, whose owners owned a seventh or ninth sheaf to their overlord but were subject to hardly any other servitude, or *terres vilaines*, whose owners owed only the eleventh sheaf but were liable to many other distressing exactions.

The loss of Normandy induced King John to forbid the exportation of any insular produce or revenues from the Islands to the Continent, so that to the royal camparts and windmill[1] were added the revenues, *esperquerie* and water-mill belonging to the Bishop of Coutances. After this time the Bishop's Court gradually lapsed, or became inferior to the King's Court, in which it was entirely merged when all the property belonging to alien priories was confiscated by Henry IV.

After 1320 the senior jurat, and not the Prévôt, presided over the Court, and was called the Judge, or rather Juge-Délégué, meaning that he was the delegate of the Bailiff of the Guernsey Court, to which the Court of Alderney has always been subordinate, having only a limited jurisdiction in civil cases, and none at all in criminal cases.

In early times the King apparently farmed or gave away his rights in Alderney, for in the twelfth century

---

[1] In 1309 there were also "two free hand-mills" in the island belonging to Nicholas le Neir and Sampson le Conte.

"The Key of the Channel"

William Artifex—or, as French historians call him, Guillaume l'Ingenieur—is described as being "Lord of Alderney" and as a donor of money and lands in that island to the church of Notre-Dame-du-Vœu at Cherbourg. These rights, however, Peter and Magnerus Ingeniator, sons of William, quit-claimed to King Henry II. for £10 sterling on November 19, 1238. The de Barentins also owned some Alderney property, but conveyed it to Richard de Gray, guardian of the Islands in 1226 and 1229, in exchange for the Fief Paisnel in Jersey. These lands subsequently lapsed to the King, for we find that in 1309 the whole commonalty of Alderney were amerced for attempting to defraud His Majesty of their revenues. In 1376 Edward III. leased Alderney for three years to Thomas Portman, a merchant of Salisbury, at the rate of £20 a year.

The south-eastern portion of the island, just above Longy Bay, appears to have been the earliest inhabited part. In the neighbourhood of its dolmens the first fishing hamlet or town of Alderney was built. This town must have been "the vill of St. Mary," of which we read in the Assize Roll of 1309;[1] and to St. Mary Alderney's earliest church was dedicated, for in a charter of 1134[2] the canons of Cherbourg and Humfrey de Ansgerville notify that they have restored the church of "St. Mary of Alderney" to the Bishop and Chapter of Coutances.

The conversion of the island to Christianity is traditionally supposed to have been accomplished by a disciple

[1] Pp. 335-6.   [2] Round's *Calendar*, pp. 342-3.

of St. Magloire, the Breton saint Guennolé or Vignalis, who probably founded one or more of the ancient chapels which have long since disappeared, though their names have come down to us as St. Barbe, St. Nicholas, St. Clair, St. Michel, and St. Aichadrius or Esquerre, the last being situated north of Longy Bay and probably identical with the St. " Deharii " mentioned in the Assize Roll of 1309 as being " next the castle " and belonging to the King.   For on Longy heights stood a castle of which the remains still exist, though this building, which once so proudly defended the island and sheltered its governors, has long been allowed to fall into ruin.   At the beginning of the last century the remains of four dungeons, situated at each corner of the building, could still be seen.   In 1812 John le Mesurier, then Governor of the island, turned the whole enclosure into a sheep-fold, and, while destroying much of the ancient masonry, built the little domed tower which is still to be seen. Situated on rising ground and surrounded by walls, it was originally called the Murs de Haut; but either the purchase of Alderney in 1590 by Queen Elizabeth's favourite, the Earl of Essex, or its having been the residence of Sir William Essex when Governor of the island in the seventeenth century, gained for this structure its present name of Essex Castle.   There is no evidence but tradition to show that Lord Essex ever landed in the island, and his purchase of it is thus accounted for by an old writer : [1] " És dernières guerres le Comte d'Essex alla

---

[1] MSS. written between the years 1620 and 1640 by Elie Brevint, minister of Sark, and transcribed by the Rev. George Lee.

contre Rouen, and Sir Th. Leighton[1] qui avoit autrefois veu la ville fut appellé pour estre de son conseil, et un Chamberlan, frère puisné de celui qui estoit Capitaine de Guernezé avant Sir Th. Leighton estoit vivandier de l'armée du Comte; et parce qu'il n'y pouvoit fournir [? provisions] il vendit ou engages Aurigni, duquel il estoit Seigneur, pour mille Livres sterlings à un sien parent, lequel parent par authorité du Comte fut mis en possession de la dite Isle pour l'espace de vingt ans, et en jouit encore à présent. Soit que le terme ne soit encore expiré, soit que la Damoiselle es mains de laquelle le droict du Comte est devolu, luy ait confirmé le don ou possession ou autrement."

According to the writer of a little book about Alderney,[2] one of the articles of impeachment against Lord Essex set forth that his design in buying the island " was to secure the person of Elizabeth in this isolated and fortified spot, in order to compel her, amongst many other matters, to settle the succession to her Crown upon him, and, in case of her refusal, himself to assume the reins of government." Below this castle and near Longy Bay is another old building, now called the " Nunnery," but figuring in ancient documents as Les Murs de Bas. According to the MSS. of the late Mr. I. A. le Coq, Judge of Alderney, it dates from the year 1436, when it

---

[1] Then Governor of Guernsey.

[2] *The Island of Alderney*, by Louisa Lane-Clarke (Guernsey), 1851. The authoress was descended from the le Mesuriers, hereditary Governors of Alderney, and claimed the authority of family manuscripts for many of her statements.

was erected as a blockhouse by the English Government. Dr. Lukis describes it[1] as of "a quadrangular form, with remains of corner towers having a circular base. These towers are about six feet in diameter, formed of very solid masonry three feet thick. At the height of seventeen feet from the ground the courses are continued in the herring-bone work, composed of stone and Roman tiles. . . . The structure, evidently raised with the materials derived from the Roman town situate at a short distance from its walls, was restored for the accommodation of troops in the year 1793, when its present entrance was constructed. . . ." The "Castrum Longini," or "Château de Longis," is set down in Leland's diminutive map.

This building is said to have communicated with the castle above by means of a subterranean passage. It was rebuilt in 1584-5 by the orders of John Chamberlain, Seigneur of Alderney, probably with a view to residing there. William Chamberlain wrote to the Privy Council in 1608 that the old castle was no longer serviceable for the defence of the island; that a small house, which had in former days served as a refuge for pirates and adventurers, had recently been repaired and used as a guard-house; and that another fort, also in ruins, was equally in need of repair.[2]

The low-lying town once situated in this vicinity and probably the church were some centuries ago overwhelmed by an inundation of sand, the result of some

[1] *British Archæological Journal*, 1847.
[2] Dupont, iii., p. 660.

terrific storm.   The precise date of this inundation is unknown, but a document known as the "Vieux Rental" of Alderney dated 1572, when treating of the wages due to the King's *sergent*, mentions that among his dues was "un costill à la Vallette d'Herbage appellée le costill au dit sergent, contenant iii. vergées ou environ, mais n'est point relevé, ce clos estant submergé par les sablons aussi bien que les terres d'autour au ouest du fort ou montagne de Longy"—which leads to the inference that the inundation had taken place within some measurable distance of time before 1572.   But in spite of the destruction of the town—whatever town there may have been—the tiny harbour at Longy continued to be the only port of the island until 1736, when Governor le Mesurier at his own expense built a small breakwater on the northern side of the island.   Heylyn, writing in 1629, says: "A great quantity of this little island is overlaid with sand, driven by the fury of the north-west winds; if we believe their legends, it proceeded from the just judgment of God upon the owner of those grounds, who once (but when, I know not) had made booty, and put unto the sword some certain Spaniards there shipwrecked."

The granite blocks scattered on the uplands of Les Rochers, but having no adherence to the soil, have by some been considered to be fragments of this submerged town.

The inhabitants who survived this catastrophe retreated to the heights in the centre of the island and proceeded to found their new settlement at Le Bourgage, the nucleus of the present town of St. Anne.[1] There also, on the foundations of a ruined chapel, they erected the first church, dedicated to St. Anne, which must originally have been very primitive, for the nave and north side-chapel were not built until 1761, nor the tower at the east end until 1767. This old church was allowed to fall into a state of hopeless dilapidation, and, with the exception of the clock tower, was finally pulled down. The present beautiful church, designed by Sir Gilbert Scott, was erected in 1850 by the Rev. John le Mesurier, son of the last hereditary Governor of Alderney, in memory of his parents.

In the thirteenth, fourteenth, and fifteenth centuries Alderney, by reason of its proximity to France, suffered even more than the other islands from the ravages of French and other marauders, and finally in 1558 it was taken by a Captain Malesart of Cherbourg and his band of adventurers. Among them was the Sire de Gouberville, who has left a journal, quoted by Dupont,[2] recounting the event, and describing how " le dymanche troys (juillet) toute la compagnée ne bougea de l'isle et y fismes grand chère. Je disne chez le Capitaine Malesart et

---

[1] It has been a subject of discussion whether the St. Anne to whom the church and the town of Alderney is dedicated is the ordinary St. Anne of Catholic hagiology, the mother of the Virgin, or the Breton St. Anne, mother of St. Sampson and aunt of St. Magloire. As both Normans and Bretons, as well as naming each homestead after its respective owner, almost invariably named their churches after their founders or after purely local saints, the balance of opinion is in favour of the latter theory.

[2] Vol. iii., p. 336.

souppe chez le sieur de Sideville. Tous les jours nous nous pourmenasmes par l'isle pour voyer les descentes qui y sont et visiter les forts."

But the English fleet under Admiral Clinton was not far off, and he and his men, assisted by Sir Leonard Chamberlain, the Governor of Guernsey, reconquered the island and made most of the Frenchmen prisoners. As a reward, in the following year Queen Elizabeth granted Alderney to Sir Leonard's son, George Chamberlain. By Letters Patent dated 1584, in consideration that " the Island of Alderney, within her Majesty's Duchy of Normandy, had lain waste and been uninhabited by her Majesty's subjects, and turned to no profit and been resorted to by enemies, Pirates and Robbers," the Queen granted it, with all its rights and emoluments, to " John Chamberlain, his heirs and assigns, for ever, *in capite*, by a knight's fee," with the proviso that he should cause it to be inhabited by at least forty of her subjects. It was apparently this John Chamberlain who in 1590 transferred Alderney to William Chamberlain, whom we afterwards find involved in the first of the many disputes between the seigneurs and the wild and lawless inhabitants of the island.

In the reign of Elizabeth, Alderney threw off the yoke of Roman Catholicism, and the Extent of 1607 computes the value of the " rents escheated which have been given to the maintenance of Superstitions and Abuses" as about four quarters of wheat and £26 sterling in money. But Protestantism was not encouraged by the Chamberlains, who were bigoted Roman Catholics. Sir Leonard

The Channel Islands

was the Governor of Guernsey when three unfortunate women were burnt for heresy;[1] and Sir Leonard's grandson, George Chamberlain, as Bishop of Ypres from 1626 to 1634 was the immediate predecessor of the famous Cornelius Jansen.[2] It is not altogether surprising, therefore, that in 1609 we find the inhabitants, "weary to live in such unchristian and barbarous estate," complaining to the Royal Commissioners that the living of Alderney had been left vacant for sixteen years, and that to their great inconvenience they had been obliged to come all the way to Guernsey for their marriages and their baptisms.

This Romish bias on the part of its Governors probably led to Alderney's being reclaimed by the Crown, and after a short rule by Sir William Essex it was included in the jurisdiction of the Governors of Guernsey.

But the Chamberlains evidently did not immediately vacate the island, for a memorandum in the State Paper Office, supposed to date from 1643,[3] says: "There is one called Chamberlain, a fermer of the Iland of Olderney, who is estimed among the better sort of the inhabitants of Garnesey to be a great Papist, and to send secretly men over into France with advises." This probably explains the stringency of an order which Robert Russell, Parliamentarian Governor of Guernsey, gave in 1643, to his lieutenant in Alderney, Pierre le Febvre, Seigneur de l'Espine. "Vous prendrez garde," he wrote,[4] "que les Papistes ou Catholiques Romains

[1] *Ante.*   [2] *Notes and Queries,* Third Series, vi., 403.
[3] *Ibid.,* vi., 331.   [4] Syvret MSS.

soient chassés, que aucun qui auroit tenu tant soit peu
d'inclination pour adhérer à superstition ne soit aucune-
ment souffert dans la ditte Isle."

A few weeks before the Restoration, Charles II.
granted the island to Edward de Carteret of Jersey, and
this grant he confirmed in August 1660, including,
however, James de Carteret and Clement le Couteur as
objects of his bounty. These three men were given
Alderney for thirteen shillings annual rent, and were to
hold it conjointly until the death of the last survivor, but
in the autumn of the same year they sold their rights to
Sir George Carteret. A little over twenty years later Sir
George's widow and heirs sold the remainder of their
lease to Sir Edmund Andros, and in consideration of the
latter's having voluntarily resigned his rights to the
Crown, a fresh Patent was issued, granting Alderney at
the same rent as before to him and his heirs for ninety-
nine years. On his death without issue in 1705, Sir
Edmund bequeathed the island to his nephew George
Andros, who died the following year, leaving as his heirs
his sister Anne, wife of John le Mesurier, and two
daughters who both died minors and unmarried; and
thus it passed into the hands of the le Mesurier family.

In 1763 John le Mesurier, then Governor, obtained
the renewal of his lease for another term of ninety-nine
years, and he and his family, enriched as they were by
their successful privateers, spent large sums of money,
and did all in their power to improve the island, civilise
the people, and reorganise the militia.

Prior to 1777 the defence of the island was chiefly

committed to the vigilance of women. As Mrs. Lane-Clarke tells us,[1] " there were beacon towers and a watch-house in different parts of the island, and here the women watched whilst the men laboured at their usual avocations. On these mounds were placed tar-barrels, heaped over with fern, and when an alarm was given they were fired as signals to the neighbouring island. The dress of the Alderney women was peculiar, consisting of a scarlet cloth petticoat and jacket, a large ruff round their necks fastened under the chin by a black ribbon or gold hook, and a round linen cap stiffened so much as to be taken off and put on like a man's hat. It is reported that on one occasion, when the island was menaced by a French man-of-war, the Governor ordered out all the women in their scarlet dresses, and, disposing them skilfully upon the heights, effectually deceived the enemy with the appearance of his forces."

During the eighteenth century the conquest of England was fully determined by the French, and the capture of the Channel Islands was decided to be the first step to this end. Even de Rullecourt's defeat in Jersey in 1781 did not discourage them, and in 1794 over 20,000 men were under arms at St. Malo, and Alderney was resolved upon as the port of debarkation.[2] But the French armament was defective, and their plans so badly laid that the English Admiral, through an intercepted letter, got wind of their project, and thus the

---

[1] *Alderney*, p. 85.

[2] *Projets et Tentatives de Debarquement aux Iles Britanniques*, by Edouard Desbrière, t. i., p. 37.

attempt had to be abandoned, although the northern ports of St. Malo, Havre, and Cherbourg continued to be strongly garrisoned and fortified.

As a reply to these menaces England resolved to strengthen the defences of all the Islands, and especially of Alderney. Since that time successive Governments have spent millions of money in building huge forts around the Islands; but many of these, being of no use for modern warfare, have been allowed to fall into ruins. The island became so important in the estimation of England that in 1825 John le Mesurier, in a fit of pique at the ingratitude of the people, surrendered his patent to the Crown in consideration of the payment of £700 a year during the residue of the ninety-nine years' term, and from that date Alderney has been under the administration of the Lieutenant-Governors of Guernsey, while the revenues hitherto belonging to the hereditary Governors were received, until quite recently, by the Office of Woods. They have now been given back to the insular authorities and a new Constitution has been inaugurated under the auspices of Sir John Capper, Lieutenant-Governor of Guernsey.

The appearance of Alderney from the sea is that of a rugged mass of solid granite, covered with a flat carpet of green, and rent by giant fissures running down to the sea. It is surrounded by dangerous rocks and whirl-pools, between which rushes a seething tide, and the plaintive cries of countless sea-birds seem a fitting accompaniment to the dreary aspect of the grim rocks and foaming sea. The first impression on landing is that of desolation and ruin. Half of the breakwater which was erected at enormous expense in 1847 has been swept away by the sea; the houses built hard by to accommodate the army of labourers employed on these harbour-works have fallen or are falling down; the little sleepy town with its grass-grown streets is surrounded by alleys, houses, and gates all mouldering into decay; and in the distance the ruined walls of once powerful forts stand, although their "wind-worn battlements are gone."

But when once on the beautiful southern coast, looking down on

> "The murmuring surge
> That on th' unnumber'd idle pebbles chafes,"

it is impossible not to feel that rugged, treeless Alderney has a savage, untamed beauty denied to the other islands: the beauty of wild nature, swept by sea-breezes, washed by brilliant foaming waves, and surrounded by

> "Cliffs and downs and headlands which the forward-hasting
> Flight of dawn and eve empurples and embrowns."

If the theory be true that men, like insects, are what their environment makes them, it is easy to understand how some of the gloomy ferocity of their island entered into the disposition of the lawless Alderney wreckers, pirates, and freebooters of former days, who, cut off by their perilous seas from much intercourse with the outer world, retained their primitive beliefs and superstitions until a comparatively late period. Mrs. Lane-Clarke,[1]

[1] *Alderney*, pp. 50-1.

CHAPTER XIII

THE "GARDEN OF CYMODOCE"

THE old legends of enchanted islands, which appear at one time almost within reach and at another far away on the horizon, are irresistibly recalled as one gazes at Sark from Guernsey. On some days it is so clear-cut against the sky that every undulation is visible; on others, so shrouded in dim mists that it seems long miles away.

At first sight it looks almost inaccessible, for its rock-bound shores—where on every peak and headland gorse blazes golden against the sky—rise sheer three hundred feet above the sea. Not until half the circuit of the island has been made does the little harbour, with its modern pier and breakwater, come into sight. In former days only the sloping beach at Le Creux and the little artificially hewn tunnel gave access to this " small, sweet world of wave-encompassed wonder." [1]

This "Garden of Cymodoce," as Mr. Swinburne called it, is by far the loveliest and least spoilt of the Islands—

---

[1] The memory still survives of the occasion when the Lords of the Admiralty, wishing to land and inspect the defences of Sark before the harbour was built, sailed round and round the island vainly seeking for a landing-place, and finally sailed away, declaring that it was inaccessible.

a tableland surrounded and upheld by wild beetling cliffs and intersected by cool green country roads leading to old thatched granite farmhouses. This verdant plateau slopes everywhere into wooded valleys, which in springtime are so thick with primroses or with wild hyacinths that the ground seems flooded with pale golden light, or is blue as if with " the heavens uprising through the earth"; and these glades end abruptly in some rocky precipice, which, right down to the water's edge, is fringed with ferns, heather, and ivy, or set with clusters of sea campion, fragile and white as the spray itself. At the foot of these cliffs the coast is in many places broken up into caves, which are almost as much a feast of colour as the land above, filled as they are with dark pools and purple rocks covered with countless seaweeds, and containing such an infinite variety of sea-anemones that they are

" From the crown of the culminant arch to the floor of the lakelet
　　abloom,
　One infinite blossom of blossoms innumerable aflush through the
　　gloom."

Great Sark is connected with Little Sark by " one sheer thread of narrowing precipice " called the Coupée. Far below the sea thunders and roars; it is the wildest, weirdest spot in the Channel Islands. Especially is its grandeur enchanced when the surroundings are obscured by drifting masses of rainclouds or wreaths of fog, when the sea murmurs invisible beneath and the really great depth seems illimitable, and, standing on the narrow causeway, one seems to have wandered somehow into space and to be surrounded by nothing but the elementary forces of nature.

This little isolated rock in the Channel has had a varied and eventful history.[1] Like the other islands, it was populated in the dim past by the dolmen-builders, though the evidences of their occupation have now mostly been destroyed. Other relics of ancient peoples are still found in the island, such as stone celts, known to the peasantry as *coins de foudre* or thunderbolts, and regarded as talismans against lightning; stone discs or amulets called *rouette des fêtiaux*, or fairies' spinning-wheels; and tiny pipes with very small bowls called *pipes des fêtiaux*, or fairies' pipes—for in Sark, as in Normandy and Brittany, everything old and mysterious is associated by the simple country folk with "the fairies," a lingering belief in whom still survives.

The earliest known inhabitants of Sark in historic times were probably a detachment of the Visigothic army. For we read in the proceedings of the Sark Court for 1718 that five Sarkese declared upon oath that in making a hedge they found in an earthen pot bound with an iron hoop thirteen pieces of metal, twelve of them shaped like plates but of different sizes, and the other oblong and in the form of a fish, which were identified as specimens of the Mint of Catoluca[2] (con-

---

[1] Much use has been made in this chapter of the Rev. J. L. V. Cachemaille's *History and Descriptive Sketch of the Island of Sark*, which appeared in Clarke's *Guernsey Magazine* for the years 1874, 1875, and 1876.

[2] *The Sark Guide*, by G. W. James (Guernsey, 1845).

jectured to be the place now called Cadillac) in the Visigothic kingdom; also eighteen small coins rudely engraved with a lion, the badge of the Visigothic dynasty. From being unmixed with Frankish money of a later date, it has been conjectured that these Visigoths garrisoned or at least visited Sark about the beginning of the fifth century, almost a hundred years before the final conquest of Gaul.

The Breton missionary St. Magloire, when he first repaired to the Islands, took up his abode in Sark and founded a chapel and a monastery, the latter on the site still known as Le Moinerie, situated near Eperquerie—then the harbour of Sark—and close to a little stream, upon which a watermill was erected some eighty feet above the bay, to which it gave the name of Port-du-Moulin.

Tradition says that, in answer to an appeal for support from St. Magloire, more than sixty monks from Normandy, Brittany, and Great Britain came over to the island and founded a school which flourished until swept away by the wild northern pirates under the Danish Jarl Hastings or Hatenai. Traces of Scandinavian entrenchments are still to be seen at Grand Fort and at Le Château or Hog's Back, where so much mediæval pottery was found, besides portions of weapons and ornaments in gold and silver, when the interior of the fort was cleared.

We have seen in the preceding chapter that Sark, with Alderney, was given by William Longsword, Duke of Normandy, to the Abbey of Mont St. Michel, and

THE COUPÉE, SARK.

transferred by the Conqueror to the diocese of Avranches.

In the twelfth century we find Sark in the possession of the powerful Norman family of de Vernon, whose connection with the Islands was strengthened by the subsequent marriage of Marie, William de Vernon's daughter, to Pierre de Préaux, "Seigneur des Iles." About the year 1160 this William de Vernon granted to the Abbey of Montebourg "the chapel of St. Maglorius in Serk," as well as the site of the mill which had belonged to St. Magloire. This gift was confirmed by his son Richard de Vernon in 1196 by a charter executed and witnessed in the chapel itself. Appended to this charter is a seal representing an armed knight bearing a shield displaying a saltire—the same arms as were borne by Matilda de Vernon, wife of Richard de la Haye, the founder of the Abbey of Blanchelande. In the reign of King John the de Vernons took the part of Philip Augustus, and thus Sark became forfeit to the King of England.

It was then ravaged by that "moine devenu démon," the renegade Fleming, Eustache le Moine. This adventurer, accompanied by Geoffrey de Lucy (at one time " Seigneur des Iles," though afterwards another deserter from the service of King John), invaded the Islands in 1214; but they were finally repulsed, leaving behind as prisoners the men by whom Sark was garrisoned, including a brother and an uncle of Eustache.

In the Assize Roll of 1309 we find Nicholas, Bishop

of Avranches, and the Abbot of Montebourg disputing with the King certain rights in Sark, especially the lucrative seigneurial perquisite of a mill and the advowson of the church (presumably the chapel of St. Magloire). The advowson seems to have been awarded to the Abbot, for in 1338 Montebourg continued to send over a monk to reside in the priory and perform the services of the chapel.

In those days Sark formed a separate bailiwick, as " William, son of Richard," was then the Bailiff, and Ralph Ode—in succession to Richard Durell—was then Provost or Sheriff, while, as in Alderney, there were six jurats of the King's Court and twelve jurors of the Crown, who were probably chosen for the purpose of the Assize from among the residents.

The King had at that time, " near the Priory in front of the house of Putyball," certain lands where his grange was situated, and a rabbit warren which, in 1309, was farmed for fifty livres, "but it has never before been let for so much." [1]

There appear to have been over a dozen minor holdings, as well as the principal fiefs—namely, Collochit, Machon, Geoffrey Richard,[2] Richard Marie, and John

[1] Assize Roll, p. 202. According to the accounts of John Gaunt, Receiver, in 1352, Sark was then farmed for £50 to Bernard de St. Jean, and Pierre de St. Père.

[2] In the year 1450 and 1451, according to the accounts of Thomas Guille, Receiver of the Earl of Warwick, then " Seigneur des Iles," a certain William Richard farmed Sark at the annual rent of 63 crowns 2 sols sterling, inclusive of grazing and rabbits. He was probably a descendant of this original landowner.

The "Garden of Cymodoce"

Neel—into which Sark was then divided, the tenants of which owed "carriage of the corn of the champart of the lord the King in Normandy wheresoever the officers of the lord the King shall wish, between Mount St. Michael and Cherbourg," these tenants being obliged to provide the linen cloths and sacks as well as the boats in which the corn was transported, and to "keep the prisoners of the lord the King in the aforesaid fees."

During the fourteenth century, however, Sark was included in the many invasions the Islands suffered at the hands of the French and other foes; its farms were ravaged and its peaceful inhabitants destroyed, and it acquired the reputation of being a haunt of pirates and adventurers and of men who decoyed vessels by false beacon lights to their rocky shores, and then plundered them. These wreckers were such a menace to the trade of the Channel that in 1356 some merchants of the ports of Rye and Winchelsea fitted out a vessel for the purpose of expelling them. They are said to have succeeded in entering the island by means of a stratagem, which Sir Walter Raleigh—sometime Governor of Jersey, whence he probably derived his information—relates in his *History of the World*, though he postdates the incident by some two hundred years, and describes it as having occurred to the crew of a Flemish ship. This is his story:

"The Island of *Sark*, joining to *Guernzey*, and of that Government, was in Queen *Mary's* time surprized by the *French*, and could never have been recovered again by strong hand, having Cattle and Corn enough upon the Place to feed so many men as will serve to defend it, and being every way so inaccessible that it might be held against the *Great Turk*. Yet by the industry of a Gentleman of the *Netherlands* it was in this sort regained. He anchored in the Road with one Ship, and, pretending the Death of his Merchant, besought the *French* that they might bury their Merchant in hallowed Ground, and in the Chapel of that Isle; offering a Present to the *French* of such Commodities as they had aboard. Whereto (with Condition that they should not come ashore with any Weapon, not so much as with a Knife) the *French* yielded. Then did the *Flemings* put a coffin into their Boat, not filled with a Dead Carcass, but with Swords, Targets and Harquebuzes. The French received them at this Landing, and, searching every one of them so narrowly as they could not hide a Penknife, gave them leave to draw their Coffin up the Rocks with great difficulty. Some part of the *French* took the *Flemish* Boat, and rowed aboard their Ship to fetch the Commodities promised, and what else they pleased, but, being entered, they were taken and bound. The *Flemings* on the Land, when they had carried their Coffin into the Chapel, shut the door to them, and, taking their Weapons out of the Coffin, set upon the *French*. They ran to the Cliff, and cry to their Companions aboard the *Fleming* to come to their Succour. But, finding the Boat charged with *Flemings*, yielded themselves and the Place."

Sir Edgar MacCulloch [1] points out that though it

[1] *Guernsey Folklore*, p. 470.

GROSNEZ POINT, JERSEY—SARK IN DISTANCE.

may be rash to deny that such an event ever occurred in the history of Sark, yet from the days of the Wooden Horse of Troy similar tales have been told in many other countries, and that it is therefore quite possible that this story may be a mere survival or echo of some ancient legend. For the next two hundred years the island apparently remained uninhabited, and in 1549 a little force of eleven galleys under the command of Léon Strozzi, the Prior of Capua, sailed from France, and Captain François Bruel de Bretagne and four hundred men landed at the Eperquerie and peacefully took possession of and fortified the island. These men, who were said to have been recruited from every French prison, soon got tired of their enforced banishment, and seized every opportunity of escaping, so that, in 1553, the garrison had dwindled down to ninety men, and in consequence the island was easily recaptured by a force of some Flemish vessels under one Adrian Crole. Crole, a corsair, who was sailing under licence of the Comte de Beverin, Admiral of the Spanish fleet, came to Guernsey, and, at the instigation of Compton, Lieutenant of Sir Peter Meautis, who gave him pilots, landed in Sark. There he found the sentinels asleep and captured the garrison, then numbering about ninety. He then reported his capture to the Spanish Ambassador at the English Court, who referred the matter to the Emperor Charles, who then offered it to Queen Mary; she, feeling that the French might take offence, was not responsive to the idea of being bribed by a Spaniard with a portion of her own inheritance, and the incident became an "affaire d'État." Meanwhile, Crole, disappointed of the handsome reward he expected, sold his artillery and stores to the Lieutenant of Alderney, shook the dust of Sark off his feet, and sailed away. That December—1553—the French raised troops and recovered the island, but in the following May it was again recaptured.

After this the island again remained totally uninhabited for some years. The next chapter of its history is narrated by the anonymous author of the *Chroniques de Jersey*, who lived at that time.

It appears that Helier de Carteret, the Seigneur of St. Ouen (grandson of the Philip de Carteret and Margaret Harliston, whom we met with in an earlier chapter), seeing the danger that might arise to the other islands if this vulnerable spot was left thus unguarded, by the permission of the Guernsey authorities took possession of the island and decided to colonise and cultivate it. He had married his first cousin, Margaret de Carteret, widow of Clement Dumaresq, and, relying on her "grand courage et bon vouloir," took her over to Sark with him. They found the island a wilderness, with neither roads where a cart could pass nor a harbour where a boat could land with any safety; filled with thorns, furze, and briers, and burrowed through and through by innumerable rabbits. They were compelled to take with them meat, drink, and every other necessary of life, and Madame de Carteret, in default of any other house or habitation, was fain to take up her abode in the little vaulted chapel of St. Magloire, while her husband and his followers set about repairing and thatching with

The " Garden of Cymodoce "

Helier de Carteret having collected his tenants and got them to build his windmill, set them to work at a breakwater in the little Baie de la Motte, and bored a tunnel through the adjacent cliff (from whence it derived its present name of " creux " or hole), so that a cart-track could be made and goods conveyed from the sea-shore to the interior of the island. He also brought over from Jersey a Norman minister of the Reformed Church named Cosmé Brevint,[1] and the old chronicler in a burst of pride assures us that " n'y a Église en toutes les Isles n'y ailleurs mieux reformée, n'y où le peuple soit mieux gouverné et mieux réglé en la crainte de Dieu, qu'en celle de l'Isle de Sercq."

Sark's earliest Court was modelled on the Royal Court of Jersey, with a Bailiff, twelve jurats, a Procureur, and several minor officials, all elected from the islanders, and presided over by the seigneur. One of its earliest records, dated 1579, relates to a fine which it inflicted on five of the inhabitants for omitting to attend the evening sermon on the previous Sunday. For in those days the people spoke of "going to the sermon" and not of going to church; and the road leading west from Elie Brevint's house to the site of the old church is still called " La Rue du Sermon." This religious enthusiasm on the part of the civil authorities was somewhat incon-

---

[1] Cosmé Brevint was succeeded by his son Elie, Minister of Sark from 1612 to 1674, and uncle of Dr. Daniel Brevint, S.T.P., Dean of Lincoln and Prebendary of Durham. Elie Brevint's notebook of jottings and memoranda is in the possession of the present Seigneur of Sark.

gruous, for the Bailiff of Sark at the time was Edouard, illegitimate son of Helier de Carteret, a man who, though resolute and brave like his father, yet had led a notoriously dissolute life. But this original constitution was short-lived. In 1582 the Guernsey Court decided that as Sark formed a portion of the bailiwick its institutions should be modelled on that of the larger island, so the self-elected officials were dismissed, and the whole manner of procedure was remodelled. But the rigid Presbyterianism of this second administration led to its downfall, and in 1672 by an Order in Council[1] the Royal Court of Guernsey was ordered to appoint a seneschal, as the Sark jurats "refused to take the oaths and subscribe the Declaration, and receive the Sacrament of the Lord's Supper in such a manner as by Law directed," and they were consequently abolished.

By an Order in Council dated June 20, 1922, the administration of the island has been reconstituted, not without a certain amount of resistance on the part of its inhabitants.

A rare tract,[2] entitled *News from the Channel, or the Discovery and Perfect Description of the Isle of Serk*, being a letter from "A gentleman now inhabiting there, to his Friend and Kinsman in London," published in 1673, gives a description of the island as it then existed. The writer touches upon the "rare mutton," and the abundance of woodcock, wild duck, and "clift-Pidgeons,

[1] *Second Report of Commissioners*, 1846, p. 186.
[2] Lately republished under the auspices of the Rev. George Lee (Guernsey, 1902).

with which at some seasons the whole island is covered."
He describes the people as being "naturally of a
courteous affable temper," and of their dress, which
resembled that of the Bretons at Morlaix, he says that
every man religiously preserves " his vast blew Trunk
Breeches and a Coat almost like a Dutch Froe's Vest,
or one of your Watermen's Liveries; Nor are the Women
behindhand with them in their Hospital gowns of the
same colour, Wooden sandalls, white Stockings, and Red
Petticoats so mean they are scarce worth taking up:
both Sexes on Festivals wear large Ruffs, and the
Women instead of Hats or Hoods Truss up their hair,
the more Gentile sort in a kind of Cabbidge-net, those
of meaner Fortunes in a piece of Linnen—[which] they
tying on the top make it shew like a Turkish Turbant,
but that part of it hangs down their backs like a Veil."

Sark remained in the hands of the de Carterets until
1713, when Sir Charles de Carteret, Baronet, being
heavily in debt, obtained permission from Queen Anne
to sell the island. It then passed into the family
of Milner, and after they had held it for a few years it
was purchased in 1730 by Dame Susanne, *née* le Gros,
widow of Mr. Nicholas le Pelley.[1]

About twenty-five years later Dame Elizabeth
Etienne, widow of Mr. Daniel le Pelley, "Dame de

---

[1] She was a Sark woman, being a daughter of Mr. Jean le Gros,
" juge et Capitaine de Serc," and had married her first cousin. The
le Pelleys were of an old Guernsey family, who had formerly owned
" la grande maison et parc des Balans " in the Vale parish, and afterwards the property of le Mont Durand in St. Peter-Port.

Serk," during the minority of her son Peter, found
herself involved in a controversy with the ecclesiastical
authorities of Guernsey respecting the advowson of
Sark. In the early days of Presbyterianism, there was
no regular building set aside for the purpose of divine
worship. St. Magloire's Chapel, which had sheltered
Madame de Carteret, had been pulled down by her husband, probably as being a relic of Popery. A little later
on the seigneur, on his own initiative, gave a small
thatched building without ceiling or chimney, and
attached to the barns of the Manor Farm, to serve as
a meeting-house, and provided a Vicar and paid his
stipend out of his own pocket. In this way succeeding
seigneurs came to claim that "the Minister officiating
in Serk has always been considered by the Lord as his
Chaplain, and paid and lodged according to agreement;
and though the tenants formerly covered the Chapel,
it must be argued that besides being appropriated to
Divine Worship, it is also the Place where the Court is
held, and where the public School is kept, so that it is
probable this service was performed for these privileges." [1] Madame le Pelley therefore felt herself quite
within her rights in dismissing for misconduct the then
Vicar, a Frenchman called Pierre Levrier, and looking
out for a substitute. But the Dean of Guernsey and the
other clergy denied her right to interfere, and thence
resulted a virtual deadlock for two years. Elizabeth le
Pelley was a masterful woman and one not to be brow-

[1] Le Pelley MSS. in possession of the late Colonel Ernest le Pelley,
son of Mr. Ernest le Pelley, the last le Pelley Seigneur of Sark.

beaten. Determined to have her own way, she locked the church door, put the key in her pocket, and defied any authority, lay or ecclesiastical, to use the building for any purpose whatever. Citations and mandates began to arrive, summoning her to go to Guernsey and appear before the Dean's Court to answer for her conduct; but she paid no attention to them. She was then threatened with excommunication; but even that did not affect her. At the end of the year her son attained his majority, and the wrath of the authorities was directed against him, and he was ordered, on pain of " excommunication majeure," to have service duly performed in the church. In obedience to this mandate, on December 14, 1755, he sent for Jean Fevot, Rector of the Vale parish, to perform the service; but while the Prayers were being read Pierre Levrier rushed in and raised the "Clameur de Haro," which effectually stopped all further proceedings and brought the whole affair under the jurisdiction of the Royal Court, who adjudged Levrier to be in the right. Among the le Pelley manuscripts, however, is preserved a " Permit from ye Seneschal to use ye Prevost and Constables to make Levrier quit ye island." This is dated 1756, and, as in the following year, a Mr. Cayeux Deschamps was appointed by the Bishop of Winchester to the cure of the island, matters evidently resulted in a triumph for the seigneur and his mother.[1]

[1] Probably this result was due to the interference of the Bishop, who was trying to control the undesirable French proselytes from the Church of Rome who at that date flocked to the Channel Islands

The Channel Islands

In 1820 this Peter le Pelley laid the foundation stone of the present church, which was completed by his son. Dr. Pusey, who resided in Sark during his suspension from his office of preacher in Oxford, was the first to wear a surplice or perform the service in English in this building. The le Pelleys had turned the former manor-house into the vicarage, having rebuilt the Perronnerie —the old house they inherited from the le Gros family —and converted it into the seigneurie. One of their last works was the building of the girls' school on a spot exactly opposite to and closely adjoining the site of the demolished chapel founded by St. Magloire.

Some education was sadly needed to brighten the lives of the Sarkese, who, to while away the monotony of the long evenings, had instituted *veilles* (watches), when all met at some appointed house to knit, sew, sing or dance. Sometimes these assemblies degenerated into orgies of masqueraders, for, alone among the Islanders, the Sarkese disguised themselves during their revels. They also had a curious custom—probably a survival of some

---

for the purpose of occupying insular livings, and were frequently the cause of grave scandals in their parishes. Some dozen years previously the Bishop had written to the ecclesiastical authorities of Jersey that no abjurations of French priests should be received by them, and that these men " professing themselves to be converts " should at once be despatched to London, where their credentials could be verified by the principal French and English authorities. The Bishop added that they were not to be given any " introductory letters " by the insular clergy, as he attributed their arrival in his diocese " as being only a convenience for making a quick escape from France " (*La Ville de St. Helier*, p. 95).

CHAPTER XIV

THE LESSER ISLANDS

HERM

HERM is somewhat less than three miles distant from Guernsey, of which it is considered politically part and parcel, although its residents affirm that its eastern shores, which are beyond the three-mile radius, own no other jurisdiction but that of the British Government. This tiny island, which at present comprises about four hundred acres of land, was in early times the abode of monks. At first it belonged to the Abbey of Mont St. Michel, but Henry II. transferred it to the Convent of Notre-Dame-du-Vœu at Cherbourg.

As one approaches Herm, a round hole is seen in a rock near the Rosière steps, looking as if it had been artificially bored to contain the staple of a gate. Tradition says that it marks the spot where the original chapel of Herm was built, and that this was swept away in a great inundation which overwhelmed more than half of the island. The little chapel which, if tradition be true, succeeded the first one, but which may itself have been the original chapel, was built on the brow of the hill and dedicated to St. Tugual. This saint was the leader of one of those migrations of Christian Britons who, flying before the invasion of heathen Saxons, occupied the sea-coast of Armorica, overthrew the pagan worship there prevalent, and gave its new name to the Duchy of Bretagne. He founded the city of Tréguier, where he ruled as bishop with the cheerful disregard of superior authority proper to his day, and possibly he, or one of his disciples, also converted the early inhabitants of Herm. Once the principal building in the island, it is now incorporated with the out-buildings of the mansion. In 1480 a friar of Cherbourg, named Jean Guyffart, was made prior of this chapel in place of Brother Richard de la Place, and the island apparently continued to be inhabited by monkish tenants until the days when religion succumbed to the clash of conflicting creeds. At that period, according to a French writer,[1] all the Roman Catholics in the other islands who had not conformed to the new faith fled to Herm, and there attempted to hold out against an onslaught of the Calvinists. But superior numbers prevailed, the Roman Catholics were forced to capitulate, the honourable terms agreed upon were repudiated by the victors, and most of the monks, together with four hundred refugees, are said to have been slaughtered.

However, no notice of this episode is to be found in any local history, and that some at least of the friars survived is testified by Elie Brevint, who wrote in 1619: " Perrine le Brocque a veu en Gerzé des beaux pères [sic] d'Erme. En la dite Isle dans l'hermitage il y a une petite Table de pierre qu'on dit estre de marbre."

Brevint also tells us that Sir Thomas Leighton, the despotic Governor of Guernsey in the days of Elizabeth,

---

[1] *La France Illustrée*, article " Coligni," by Turgin.

The Lesser Islands

was the first of the island's Governors to appropriate Herm, which had hitherto been considered as an ecclesiastical perquisite. Sir Thomas used the island as a game preserve and stocked it with deer, pheasants, rabbits, and a special breed of swans, while its pond or *vivier*—a frequent appanage of a monastery—was famous for its carp. He beguiled the monotony of his life at Castle Cornet by shooting-parties, sailing across with his friends to the island in his private boat. On one occasion, indeed, his party terminated in a sad fatality, of which the full account is preserved among the inquests of the Royal Court.

Sir Thomas had organised a day's sport for August 18, 1587. His party consisted of Mr. Peter Carey (jurat), Mr. John Andros, and four lads—his own son Thomas Leighton, Walter St. John, the young brother-in-law of his daughter Anne Lady St. John, Peter Carey, junior, and Samuel Cartwright, possibly son of the famous Presbyterian chaplain of Castle Cornet, their tutor Mr. Isaac Daubeny, and various members of the household. It was with great reluctance that Sir Thomas had allowed the boys to go, and he only consented on condition that their tutor should accompany them, take their books, and give them the usual lessons in Herm. Accordingly they all started at daybreak, and on arrival the elders went off to hunt, and the boys did their lessons up to nine o'clock. Then their music master, Mr. Nicholas Blake, made them sing for an hour, and after a service of prayer, conducted by Mr. Daubeny, they all went to dinner. The boys then begged to be allowed to bathe, and this request of theirs was also, with some hesitation, granted, on condition that some of the elders went with them. Just as they had got into the water, however, at Belvoir Bay, poor young St. John was knocked over by a wave, and though Mr. Daubeny rushed to his assistance and hoisted him on his back, he in his turn was upset, and before the others (who complained that they were entangled in masses of seaweed) could get to their assistance, they were both drowned. Mr. Peter Carey deposed at the inquest how he had been obliged to break the sad news to the Governor, who was sleeping in his tent, having been up since 1 a.m., and who became quite overwhelmed with grief, and how the sad cortège had sailed back with the two corpses to Castle Cornet.

In the following century Herm continued to be a pleasure resort of successive Governors, for Jean de la Marche, the bigoted Puritanical divine, notes in his diary that on Sunday, August 5, 1636, the Earl of Danby was " out hunting in his Island of Herm, whither he had taken the greater part of the Gentlefolks of the Town (although by so doing they profaned the Day), and he having given his Horse the Spur, it ceased not to rear and turn round and round until it had thrown him to the Ground."

In the days of Lord Hatton, Herm was farmed to Advocate Peter Gosselin, who kept there a large flock of sheep, which, as he wrote[1] to Lord Hatton, contributed " to the manufacture of stockings and to maintaine a livelyhood to above two hundred poore people that

[1] British Museum, Add. MSS. 29555, fol. 237.

worke for me." Now Francis Greene, Lord Hatton's agent in Guernsey, had a short time before—viz., in August 1677—written a letter[1] in which he tried to get the island taken away from Mr. Gosselin, saying that "Gosselin's nonsensicall sheepegrassing trade has caused yo[r] hearde of deare and eyes[2] of phesans to be lessened above halfe."

In 1737 the "Island of Erm, other Herme or Arm, with the house thereon erected, formerly a Chapple, and all the Deer, Partridges and Rabbits" on the said island, was let to Peter Carey of Guernsey, and this lease was in 1758 renewed to his son. Mr. Elisha Dobrée notes in his Journal, "December 31, 1787, Wind south; fine day; went stag shooting." And the story has been handed down that the stags would swim over from that island—at low water a distance of about two miles—to browse on the Vale Commons, and would then swim back, being intelligent enough always to choose the proper tides.

Since that time Herm has been rented from the British Government by a succession of individuals, and at the present time by Sir Percival Perry, who has lately succeeded Mr. Compton Mackenzie, the well-known novelist, as tenant of the island. For the exigencies of the War compelled the British Government to sequester Herm, which was then leased to the West Bank of Silesia and sublet by them to H.S.H. Prince Blücher von Wahlstatt; although it must be recorded that the

---

[1] British Museum, Add. MSS. 29564, fol. 221.

[2] This is an obsolete substantive used erroneously for *nye* or *neye*, meaning a brood, or, literally, a nest.

The Channel Islands

undeviating loyalty to England of the Prince and of his son Count Lothair Blücher was acknowledged by all the competent authorities.

Herm resembles Guernsey in miniature, being flat and sandy at the north and east, and steep and precipitous at the south and west. On the coast facing Sark is a very fine " creux," through which the rising tide foams and splashes; but Herm is especially famous for its two shell beaches, of which even the shingle is entirely composed of minute fragments of shell, and which are unequalled on the British coasts for the profusion, variety, and rarity of the species to be found there.

As in the other islands, neolithic remains abound; and hidden under a veil of flowers, grass, and shells lurks, to the sensitive observer, a strange sinister influence, the influence of Elemental Powers, Powers which resent the intrusion of human personality, powers which caused a former tenant to write: "Propitiate, at all costs, the Spirit of the Island. . . ."[1]

On this island a recent Bailiff of Guernsey, Sir Peter Stafford Carey, picked up an ancient gold signet ring. This ring (which Sir Peter bequeathed to the Royal Court) was identified by its workmanship and by the arms engraved upon it—a pelican in its piety—as being the signet used by Pierre de Beauvoir, Bailiff of Guernsey from 1470 to 1479, to seal his official documents. From its size it must have been worn as a thumb ring.

[1] Mrs. Compton Mackenzie, in *Eve*, April 25, 1923.

order was in course of execution when a bystander, wanting a light for his pipe, took up one of the pieces of paper and found it was half a bank-note. Needless to say, the fire was immediately extinguished, but only four mutilated notes could be rescued from the flames. A few spade guineas have also been discovered near this spot.

In 1917 Jethou could boast that two-thirds of her inhabitants had gone to the front, as, out of her total population of three men, two were fighting in France.

One of the characteristics of the Channel Islands is the way that certain names and families become localised in one particular island or even parish; and in the same manner it has been pointed out by a recent writer[1] that the plants of the various islands differ, each containing species not to be found in the others. Thus, although little Jethou has few if any song birds, and owns hardly any of the wild flowers common to the other islands, yet it contains a yellow forget-me-not which is almost peculiar to the island, and a white pimpernel, which is found neither in the other Channel Islands nor yet on the mainland of Normandy.

Lihou

The little island of Lihou is situated at L'Erée Point on the west coast of Guernsey, with which it is connected by a rough winding causeway, nearly half a mile in length, uncovered only at low tide. The island re-

[1] *Flora of Guernsey and the Lesser Channel Islands*, by E. D. Marquand (London, 1901).

sembles Jethou in having but one habitable house and a large store of wild rabbits; but whereas Jethou is high, with rocky cliffs covered with furze and bracken, and contains some fine forest trees, Lihou consists of low-lying fields of coarse grass, or sandy banks covered with fine turf and terminating in a flat stony shore, broken here and there by large picturesque masses of rock.

It contains the ruins of the priory of St. Mary of Lihou, which was confirmed by Pope Adrian IV. in 1156 to the abbot and brethren of Mont St. Michel. A rough representation of the priory chapel is cut on a stone now built into the wall of a neighbouring farmhouse, which came, tradition says, from the site of the prior's residence. It depicts a building with a chancel and nave, and with a square tower on the north-east side of the nave. On either side of the drawing are the following letters, interpolated in the nineteenth century, "H.D.M.L.H.M. MCXIV." This rough picture fully corresponds with the structure of the church as shown by the existing ruins, and the inscription is by its owners supposed to stand for "Hellier du Mont [Prior of] Lihoumel[1] [an old form of the name Lihou], 1114," the date, according to the legendary Dédicace des Églises, of its consecration.

The abbot of Mont St. Michel and the prior of Lihou were summoned before the Assize of 1309 to answer,

---

[1] Formerly it was customary in the Islands to split up the syllables of proper names when writing initials. Thus over old doorways may be seen " J. F. L." standing for Jean Falla, or " P. M. G." for Pierre Mauger, etc.

among other charges, by what warrant they claimed " to have wreck of the sea throughout all their lands of Lyhou and the sea-coast adjoining, as well as free warren, a fishery at La Russe-mare[1] and the escheats and chattels of all the felons."

The abbot and prior alleged in reply that they had had a special Royal grant as to fishery and the wreck of the sea, always excepting the usual Kingly perquisites of silk, gold, and scarlet cloth; that they claimed their right of warren " to chase in the time of season with dog and staff without engine, after the officers of the lord the King have chased "; and that as to the chattels of the felons, if the prior's men could " lay hands more quickly upon such chattels than the men of the lord the King, then he claims to have those chattels and not otherwise."

Heylyn, writing of the lesser Channel Islands, says: " The least of them, but yet of most note, is the little islet called *Lehu* . . . neer unto those scattered rockes which are called *Les Hanwaux*, appertaining once unto the Dean but now unto the Governor. Famous for a little Oratory or Chantery there once erected and dedi-cated to the honour of the Virgin *Mary*, who by the people in those times was much sued to by the name of our lady of *Lehu*. A place long since demolished in the ruine of it, *Sed jam periere ruinæ*, but now the ruines of it are scarce visible, there being almost nothing left of it but the steeple, which serveth only as a sea-

---

[1] Rousse-Mare, Claire-Mare, and Grande-Mare were three ponds on the western shores of Guernsey, and were at one time famous for their carp. They are now drained.

marke, and to which as any of that party sail along, they strike their top sail. *Tantum religio potuit suadere*, such a religious opinion have they harboured of the place, that though the Saint be gone, the wals yet shall still be honoured."

This steeple with the surrounding ruins is said to have been blown up in 1793 by order of the Governor of Guernsey on the ground that it might prove of service to the French should it fall into their hands. But the custom of paying reverence to the once sacred spot is observed by the fisher-folk to this day.

The island remained in the possession of the Governors until early in the eighteenth century, when with Herm and Jethou it was leased to the Englishman Nowell, with a proviso that the neighbours had the right of landing on his coasts to fish and to cut the *vraic* or seaweed which is particularly abundant there, and is used by the farmers to fertilise their lands.

It then passed to Messrs. John de Havilland and William le Marchant, and thence to William's brother, Eleazar le Marchant, Lieutenant-Bailiff of Guernsey.

Mr. le Marchant bequeathed this island to his cousin, Mr. Priaulx of Montville, in the hands of one of whose descendants it still remains.

THE ECREHOUS

Off the coast of Jersey are two clusters of islands, the dangerous uninhabited rocks called the Minquiers, and the group called Ecrehous, which were, before successive encroachments by the sea, far larger and more

CASQUET ROCKS AND LIGHTHOUSE.

The Lesser Islands

important than they are now. They now consist of
Maître Ile, Blanque Ile, and Marmoutière, Blanque Ile
and Marmoutière being virtually one island except at
high water.

In 1202 these islands were given by Pierre de Préaux
to the Norman Abbey of Val Richer, and on Maître Ile
are still to be seen the ruins of the chapel he founded.
For many centuries the islands have remained comparatively deserted, and only recently there died a man
named Pinel, who had led a Crusoe-like existence on
Blanque Isle for over forty years and gained the sobriquet
of " King of the Ecrehous."

Some years ago a question arose between France and
England whether these islands were really included
within Jersey territory or whether they should be considered as neutral ground. This argument resulted in
the English flag being hoisted with an unusual amount
of ceremony upon them.

THE CASQUETS

About seven miles west of Alderney, situated in the
most dangerous part of the Channel, are the famous
Casquet Rocks, " where the carcases of many a tall ship
lie buried."

At one time the belief was current that this was the
spot where the *Blanc Nef*, with Prince William, only son
of Henry I., and his noble retinue, went down, but
modern historians think the scene of that tragedy was
more likely to have been in the neighbourhood of
Barfleur.

The Channel Islands

Not until 1723, in response to a petition from the Governor of Alderney, was the first beacon light exhibited on these dangerous rocks, and then it was but a coal fire burning upon an armourer's forge and kept in flame by bellows. But this contrivance proved sadly inadequate; wreck after wreck took place on these rocks; and in 1744 the finest battleship in the British fleet, the splendid *Victory*, with Admiral Sir John Balchen and eleven hundred men on board, was driven upon them by a furious gale, and every soul perished. In 1779 this primitive appliance was superseded by an oil light in a copper lantern, and in 1790 three lighthouses named St. Peter, St. Thomas, and Donjon respectively were built and lit by an eight-revolving Argand light, fixed on a ring and moving in circular rotation. In 1846 Bell Tower was built, the bell to be rung in a fog; and on June 14, 1849, the Rev. George Guille held the first Anglican service on the rock.

From June 1828 to June 1849 these lights were looked after by a single Alderney family named Houguez, of which the man, his wife, and his six children took turns at watching and relighting the lamps so often broken and extinguished by the sea that,

> "Mounting to the welkin's cheek,
> Dashes the fire out."

To these exiles Alderney constituted both mainland and metropolis, and the details are still recalled of a visit the eldest girl was induced to pay to her relations at St. Anne's. After a short sojourn in what to her

The Lesser Islands

was a giddy whirl of society, "aweary of this great world," she joyfully returned to her rock.

> " Too full, she said, was the world of trouble,
>   Too dense with noise of the things of earth.
> And she turned her again to replenish with double
>   Delight her desire of the things of her birth.
> For joy grows loftier in air more lonely,
>   Where only the sea's brood fain would be;
> Where only the heart may receive in it only
>   The love of the heart of the sea."

Two of the lighthouses have now been converted, one into a fog-signal station and one into a store, and the remaining tower has been fitted with a very brilliant revolving light which marks the spot where so many

> " Sons of earth
> Beat down by vengeful waves,
> Sleep beneath these obliterate stones
> In unmeasurable graves."

INDEX

225

The Channel Islands

146